D1471692

STEEL CITY PRESS

This first edition published in 2021 by Steel City Press, 9 Ravenscroft Close, Sheffield, S13 8PN. Website: www.steelcitypress.co.uk

Angel in the Shadows

ISBN 978-1-913047-26-9 (paperback)
ISBN 978-1-913047-27-6 (hardback)

CONTENTS

Chapter 1 -
Skirmish in Stuttgart

"The best way to rescue a world with hurting people is to do it one person at the time" -
Manuel Corazzari

It's an icy-cold morning in Stuttgart a couple of hours before dawn; the target of today's operation is a 10-year-old Norwegian girl called Freya. She is staying at a four-star hotel with her somewhat overweight father, a balding man with glasses wearing an impressively expensive suit which at one time used to fit him. We have located Freya in the hotel through a tracking device hidden on her father's car, then kept an eye on her daily movements with covert surveillance whilst lurking in the shadows. Neither she nor her father suspect that just minutes from now, Freya will be in my car on a German Autobahn, hurtling towards the international border at high speed.

A stooge, who is the spitting image of Dr. House from the famous TV show, is sitting in the hotel lobby. He is not just posing as a hotel guest. House stayed there last night to avoid arousing suspicions with the hotel staff. It's 7.02am; Freya and her father must have overslept slightly today. They emerge from the lift and go through the door into the hotel car park. House follows them. I'm sitting in the getaway car, an unobtrusive VW Golf parked on a side street just outside the hotel car park, waiting. The conditions are perfect. There's little traffic, few pedestrians, and other cars on the street are iced up. Nobody has a serious chance of following us.

I'd say it's a tense moment, but that's a given: every moment is tense. If something goes seriously wrong, this is the moment of maximum risk. I'm focused, my former military training brought to bear. It's critical to do everything exactly on time. The adrenaline may be coursing through my veins, but it needs to be controlled and harnessed. Adrenaline is a means to an end, helping me to set aside any irrational doubts over my strategy and brush away the natural human fear response to such a dangerous situation. There's an ever-present risk of violence, arrest, jail or death in this line of work.

Freya and her father are about to get into their car; now is the time for House to strike. "Excuse me, I think you dropped your keys?" he says in slightly broken German. The father turns to see who has asked the question. "They aren't mine", he responds. House acts confused. He stumbles over a couple more words in German, and the father tries responding in English. In the moment of embarrassed confusion that follows, a tall blonde woman has scooped Freya up and is running towards the exit of the car park. The father hears Freya crying, finally recognising that there is something not quite right. House gives him a little shove, knocking him somewhat off balance – which strictly speaking he probably shouldn't do - then sprints off behind them towards the car.

House is the last one to get in, but instead of getting in by the closest door, he goes round the car to get in the front seat. Idiot, I think, but say nothing. There'll be time for bollockings later. Doesn't he realise that we're actually in a hurry here? I click the button to lock the car doors and speed away just as the father emerges from the car park. He's too late.

The mental countdown has begun in my mind. I drive quickly, jumping a red light as there's no traffic around. The least of my worries is whether or not a camera might click me; instead, I'm reassured by the fact that nobody is following me. I park the car up at the back of a petrol station less than two miles from the hotel. It's possible that the police could be looking for my Golf within minutes. I've chosen the area because it's quiet, because I know I won't be disturbed, and especially because careful surveillance has shown me that there are no security cameras here. There's a Mercedes C-Class parked up. I ditch the Golf, leaving the keys in the car. I suppose that eventually the police will return it to the rental company, so they'll need the keys. They won't find any fingerprints anyway. I've been wearing gloves the whole time. We quickly swap vehicles, and Freya starts crying again. Not that I can blame her: the whole experience must be quite bewildering and terrifying for her. But there was no other way.

The woman is comforting the child in Norwegian, reassuring her that she's safe and that mummy is here now. The Golf had been rented in her name: if the worst had happened and we'd been stopped by the police at the start of the extraction, that fact would help them to perceive it as a domestic dispute. That's what it is, after all. We have the law and the Hague Convention on our side, but we'd rather have the child safely back where she belongs before any police involvement. "Thank you", says the woman in a pure Scandinavian accent as she senses that the moment of greatest danger has passed. Now, for the first time, she dares to believe. "Thank you so much!"

We head out onto the Autobahn. A few kilometres in front of us, we've got a scout vehicle looking out for police checkpoints. If the father has somehow managed to persuade police that this is a kidnapping and not a rescue, we don't plan on hanging around to have that discussion with them. We'll save that question for Norway.

The scout vehicle has clear instructions to contact us instantly if they see any police activity or roadblocks, so that we can head off the motorway at the next exit. Or, if we've not managed to keep an exit between us, he'll create a distraction – maybe even get himself arrested - so that we'll get through. That's why our reconnaissance has to be absolutely spot on. I need to know every Autobahn exit (or Ausfahrt – lots of Brits chuckle at the way that sounds) on my route by heart. Every alternate route is etched into my memory.

I know my Plan B, Plan C, and all the way down to Plan Z. I've developed an almost photographic memory of Stuttgart's layout. In just five days, I've had to learn the city as if I'd lived there all my life. Every day, after surveillance had finished for the day, I'd be driving around. On some missions, I'd cover a thousand miles in two days under cover as a tourist, just learning and memorising routes. I needed to know every single route to be able to navigate from any location to any other. I needed to know where the local police stations were, and which of the two choices would be safer at every junction. I might use a sat-nav to help me learn the city, but it'd be next to useless during an operation. If your sat-nav goes down, you're fucked. If the situation changes, the sat-nav doesn't know and you're fucked again. It'll always take you the quickest route, not the cleverest route. Now you're fucked whilst a happy-sounding voice tells you helpfully to "do a U-turn, do a U-turn, do a U-turn" into the path of an oncoming police car. Any military operator will tell you "never trust a sat-nav" – relying on a sat-nav is just as bad as relying on a total stranger who often turns out to be even less use than a chocolate fireguard. It's proper planning which separates the successes from the failures; the winners from the losers, the charlatans from those of us who can actually rescue children.

I've driven this route a few times already to memorise routes and get the timings right. I know that from pickup to crossing the border should take 65 minutes at this time of day. The journey is surprisingly uneventful, and we don't really have much to say to each other. I'm still in military mode, caring more about my client's safety and security than chit-chat in any case. By now, no doubt the police are aware of what's going on. Think about it for a moment though. First, they'll try to trace the Golf. That was rented in France, so it might not be too easy for them to track down. If anything though, we want them to find the Golf. It's a delaying tactic. They'll be asking all sorts of questions, but our plan leads them to ask the wrong ones. Who is House? Who booked his hotel room? Who rented the Golf? Can we find any fingerprints? It's unlikely that they'll have any connection to be able to find the Mercedes C-Class – but even if they did, that's been rented in Belgium by the owner of the company I'm working for.

The police have just 65 minutes to solve the whole mystery and intercept us before we reach the border. That'll take some doing, assuming that the father even bothers to call the police. He might not even do that: he knows perfectly well that he's the one in breach of a court order, not us. If he calls the police, he's got to tell them "my ex has just taken my child". He's got to explain the situation, somehow convince them that he's right, and in that time we're already well on our way. If anything, the biggest concern is that a passer-by will think they've seen a kidnapping not a rescue and call the equivalent of 999. Still, we take no risks. From my experience of working in the military, it's always best to plan for the worst-case scenario. Our plans are designed to succeed – even if German police were to launch a national manhunt within minutes.

Halfway to Brussels, on the Franco-German border (not that the word "border" means much in the Schengen Area these days, with people and goods flowing freely across without presence or checks) there is a small railway station. It's secluded, not quite abandoned - but barely a train stops there any more.

It's the ideal place for us to transfer to our third and final car, because it's so small that there are no CCTV cameras. On the off chance that we'd made a mistake about the safety of the Mercedes, we'll be in France in an Audi A5 within seconds. Once in France, of course, German police have no jurisdiction. This isn't the quickest route to

Brussels from Stuttgart, but it's the one that gets us out of Germany in relative safety.

If anything goes wrong now, it's an international incident. If the French authorities have to determine whether Freya is returned to her father or mother, to Germany or Norway, her mother will win. Eventually. But it'll be messy. Far better to get her back to safety and avoid all kinds of complications.

We've built so much protective redundancy into the system. Murphy's Law states that "if anything can go wrong, it will", but the Army version is "if a plan is going to plan, it's probably an ambush". We look around the station area twice. The Audi is there, but the scout vehicle isn't. A phone call later, it turns out that Henrik has somehow managed to manoeuvre his scout vehicle behind us instead of in front of us. I don't know what he thought he was scouting, but he clearly wasn't. There's a hesitant, almost comical, wait as we sit around until it finally shows up. There's no time to give the driver, a Swedish guy called Henrik who is built like a Viking, a proper bollocking. We get into the Audi and cross the border.

If you've driven through France regularly, you'll know all about the long, narrow and expensive automated toll booths which charge you through the nose for the privilege of driving through France. Highway robbery perhaps, but the worst part is how temperamental the booths are. If the machine refuses to accept your toll payment, you've got to reverse carefully down the narrow yellow lanes.

Today, of course, it happens. To us. We hit a toll booth somewhere around Metz and the machine won't accept our payment. Worse still, there are two cars behind us as I back out. They have to reverse too and head for another booth, creating a bit of a commotion. Just as we manage to negotiate our way out of the lane, there are two French Gendarmes in a car behind us in the rear view mirror. They gesture to us to pull over, quite reasonably wanting to know who is driving backwards out of one of their toll booths – and why. Of all the things that can go wrong with a plan, it's the random ones which are the hardest to prepare for. Anyone can be stopped by police at any time I suppose, but truly random occurrences are naturally unpredictable.

We show our passports and documentation, and fortunately they don't ask too many more questions before we're permitted to head across the border without further incident to Belgium. I make a mental note that the next time my work takes me through France, I'll make sure to have an electronic toll pass. The elimination of unnecessary risk is my business.

The fastest route from here to Brussels would pass through the small landlocked country of Luxembourg, but there's no reason to complicate matters by crossing an extra international border. Our route keeps us in France for a while longer before we head into Belgium. The remainder of our journey to the Norwegian consulate in Brussels passes without incident. They need to go to the consulate because they don't have any form of photo identification for the child.

That's the point where what we've done needs to be spot on legally. I pull up outside and take my client inside the embassy. She sits with her child, behind a glass screen, and has to explain in detail everything that's happened. Fortunately both Germany and Norway are part of the Hague Convention, so she's able to show them all the paperwork including court documents and a return order under the Hague

Convention. Although Norway isn't in the European Union, it is in the Schengen Area. It's perfectly possible to travel from Belgium to Norway without a passport, but not by plane. For security reasons they'll need identification, and the simplest way of doing that is to get an emergency passport. It's surprisingly efficient, and we're back out of there clutching a bright orange Naudpass, replete with the Norwegian coat of arms – a lion clutching an axe on a shield - in under an hour.

The last leg of the journey, escorting mother and child to the airport, is more routine. We might not be truly relaxed, but there's no longer a sense of imminent danger. The job becomes little more than a standard personal protection detail, and once that's over we're finally able to breathe a sigh of relief.

We've just transformed a family's life. But there's no celebration, no going out for a meal and a few drinks afterwards. No need to be seen with anyone else on the team for any longer than strictly necessary. We sort out the remaining admin and finances, then vanish into the mist as we head back to our own homes. It's a bit of an anti-climax. I've just rescued a kid, but it's quite possible that I might never speak to either mother or child again.

After the adrenaline rush, it's back to normality. That's not the easiest adjustment, but I do know that my wife is missing me. Though she's wonderfully supportive of the work I do, every time I leave she knows that there's a chance I won't be coming back. I could be killed or imprisoned on trumped-up charges, and it could be months before she finds out what has happened.

THE HAGUE CONVENTION

THE HAGUE CONVENTION ON THE CIVIL ASPECTS OF INTERNATIONAL CHILD ABDUCTION (Concluded 25 October 1980)

Article 1

The objects of the present Convention are -

a) to secure the prompt return of children wrongfully removed to or retained in any Contracting State; and

b) to ensure that rights of custody and of access under the law of one Contracting State are effectively respected in the other Contracting States.

Article 3

The removal or the retention of a child is to be considered wrongful where -

a) it is in breach of rights of custody attributed to a person, an institution or any other body, either jointly or alone, under the law of the State in which the child was habitually resident immediately before the removal or retention; and

b) at the time of removal or retention those rights were actually exercised, either jointly or alone, or would have been so exercised but for the removal or retention.

Chapter 2 -
The ethics of child rescue

"To discover your mission and put it into action - instead of worrying on the sidelines - is to find peace of mind and a heart full of love" - Scilla Elworthy

Everything in this book is true, or at least as true as I can make it without putting actual people's safety at risk. I've changed names, ages, even gender sometimes. First and foremost, before anything else, I need to keep people safe. That's what this job is all about. I'm writing under a pseudonym of course, for the same reason. Nobody's ever known the truth about me. It's all been about deception. They don't know my real name, the real place I'm living, or anything else. It's the best way of keeping me and my loved ones safe.

This book is also the reality. That reality isn't always going to be pretty, and I'm not about to apologise for that because the criminals who steal kids away from loving parents don't leave much option for everything to be all nicey-nicey. If you've got any questions, or qualms, let's challenge them head-on before you read any further. Don't worry, I'm sure I've heard it all before. I'm not going to spend the rest of this book justifying how my career helps children, but I'll answer the main questions – to set your mind at rest. So that you understand.

Isn't what you do just causing trauma to kids?

I've heard that question asked many times, and the answer is 'no'! Most of them have been psychologically abused. Sometimes the person who's stolen the kid is a sexual predator, other times they're a fucking terrorist. The courts know that a child is being used as a weapon, as a pawn in an attempt to traumatise a husband or wife, or for financial gain. The Hague uses the slightly colder, dispassionate term 'left-behind parent' to describe this situation. Parents aren't trying to get their kids back out of spite. They're trying to be reunited with their loved ones, and trying to save them from a weird collection of nutters and abusers. One of them fled to Japan because he believed there was going to be a nuclear disaster leading to the end of the world. I mean yeah, whatever - but why Japan? Conveniently, Japan happened to be a safe haven for people who kidnap their children because there's no extradition treaty. We found him and we got the child back.

In the Stuttgart case, a father kidnapped his child from Norway, took the child to Germany and refused to go back. It was a crime under the Hague convention. A distraught mother hired us to get the child back.

Remember that they're on the run. There's trauma for those children on a daily basis when they've been carried off by a parent against their will. What we do gets that trauma to stop.

When we rescue a child, it's always the parent who runs through and grabs the child. There's a loving, caring presence right at the centre of everything. Initially there might be a panic, yes, but within thirty seconds they've realised it's being done to help them. Most of the time we'll do it very covertly because the parent will have some form of access to the child. That way, there isn't even that sudden element of surprise for the child. Unfortunately, when a child has been kidnapped and sent across international boundaries, it's not always possible to do it in a very calming and simple way. But especially when a parent has deliberately moved their child to a country without an extradition treaty, which isn't bound by the Hague Convention, what else can you do?

Isn't what you do kidnapping too though?

The parent has every right, both legal and moral, to go and get their child back. What they lack is the skill and expertise to do that – especially when they have an abusive ex-partner. It's the parent, not me, that's taking the child. It's always the parent who picks their child up. *We never touch a child.* I can't stress that enough, but it's a rule that we always follow. There are plenty of cowboy operators out there who play fast and loose with the rules, but it is the parent who is recovering their child – not me. I'm merely providing the operation which enables them to do it.

Rescuing a child isn't kidnapping, any more than a soldier is a murderer. A soldier has rules of engagement to govern when he can and can't fire on the enemy. Likewise, I operate based upon the documentation that I've seen, read and studied from courts of law.

I'm a reset button. I restore the status quo that existed before a parent (or even step-parent) decided to abduct a child. Getting a court order to say that a child should be returned is the easy part. Enforcing it is next to impossible, and the legal bills will mount up until they're running to the hundreds of thousands of pounds. We simply put the child back to where the child is supposed to be.

Aren't you profiting from people's misery?

I try everything in my power not to profit from people's misery. That's part of the reason I set up in business. I've got nothing but contempt for the people who prey on devastated parents who are desperate to get their children back.

When I'm on a job, I rarely stay in a hotel. I'll work until I need to sleep, then I'll sleep in my car. That's partly to keep costs low, but also because it allows me to work the absolute maximum number of hours possible. I need to be on top of everything. I'll often drive a thousand miles in two days, just to get a complete overview of every possible route within a city.

I try to charge as little as I possibly can. I need to live and to provide for my family. I don't need luxury. Eventually I'd love to eliminate fees altogether, with charitable-style donations or crowdfunding from the public to enable us to run the service free of charge.

Is it even legal?

Yes – mostly. No two countries have absolutely identical legal systems, so the actions which are legal depends on the country. On the other hand, the Hague Convention on international child abduction is binding on all 101 countries which are signed up to it.

There are sometimes some grey areas, especially in countries which aren't part of the Hague Convention, and there are certainly times when

I don't want to stick around for questioning. That's just a consequence of taking action to fix a delicate situation. And yes, there are probably a few countries where I wouldn't exactly be welcomed if I showed up at the border after having rescued a child from there. But that's a price worth paying for reuniting children with their loving families.

Can it possibly be moral, or ethical, for someone to be able to get away with kidnapping a child by crossing into a country which isn't a signatory to the Hague Convention? I don't believe that should be the case – and that's why, as a military operator, I'm willing to cross those lines when necessary. Gender isn't an issue to us; we'll rescue a kidnapped child whether the father or the mother is the one doing the kidnapping. But it can be an issue in some countries' legal systems. When a man kidnaps a child, they'll often take that child out of a legal system where men and women are treated equally, to a country where the law automatically favours a man over a woman. We don't live in a perfect world where everything all fits into a nice cosy pattern. We live in one where situations rarely neat and almost never crystal-clear.

But if you're asking questions about legality, I've got a question for you. The main story in this book is about Lebanon. At the time of writing, to the best of my knowledge I'm the only person in this line of work who has ever successfully extracted a kidnapped child from Lebanon. When someone has kidnapped your child and taken them to live with Hezbollah terrorists, what else are you going to do? If you were in that same situation, I can promise you that you would be straight on the phone to me.

Could you just be returning a child to an abuser?

I want to say an absolute clear, firm, categorical 'no'. For every case I check the court records from the custody battle. If there's the slightest hint of abuse, I refuse to take on the case. If there hasn't been a court case yet, such as when an ex takes their child on holiday and just never comes back, then I send the person concerned to obtain a return order under the Hague Convention first (and ideally an Interpol yellow notice) before I'll get involved.

There are plenty of other red flags. If the parent from whom the child was taken has been arrested for a violent offence, on principle I refuse to take on the case. There's far more information available on these parents than there would be on the average member of the public because it's gone through a whole court process already. If something just "feels" wrong, dodgy or underhand, I won't take on the case either. So I'd love to say that there's absolutely zero chance that someone's going to be sent to the wrong place, though there's no such thing as absolute certainties: there's always a tiny one-in-a-million possibility chance of something being amiss, which is why I'm constantly on the lookout for anything that's not right.

Don't get me wrong, I get the wrong people getting in touch with me all the time. I just turn down their requests for help. Sadly, there have been situations where others in this line of work have taken on some seriously questionable cases. One of my competitors (and I'll do him the courtesy of not publicly naming and shaming him in this book) effectively ended up facilitating a child abduction. A parent who hadn't seen or shown any interest in his child since the kid was a week old decided to take the child without any legal documentation. Their company didn't do any checks and took the money. They slammed the mother to the ground, in balaclavas, and drove that child to a father who the child had never met.

I got called in to fix the mess that my competitor had created, but that was easily sorted once I had chased him around Turkey and tracked him down. His actions were so illegal that we got all his assets frozen. There's often more than one way to fix a situation: he returned the child quickly enough.

Why did you set up your own company?

The complete lack of ethical standards in the business bothers me. A lot. When someone takes an extortionate sum of money from a family, knowing full well that there's no chance of success, and uses the money to fund a lavish five-star hotel lifestyle, there's a level of corruption that I'm going to run away from. When I realised that I'd been sent on an impossible mission, merely so that a client could be given a large bill, it was time to leave and steer clear of such exploitation. The only way to be sure that I was actually doing good, not harm, was to make sure I can double-check the ethics of every job.

The other big reason is total incompetence. The weakest link in any organisation is the people you're working with. The Stuttgart operation may have worked well in the end, but it was a mess. A couple of days earlier, there had been an attempt to recover Freya which had failed because 'House' failed to make the call to warn us that they were leaving the hotel. The bottom line was that he'd bottled it. Father and daughter disappeared for two days and we had to track them all over again. Then there was the fuck-up when Henrik somehow ended up behind us in the scout vehicle. I need to know that the people I'm working with aren't complete fucking idiots. They sent House to do that job because he knew karate. What the fuck has that got to do with a military operation? Having my own business, I can hire my own people. People who I know and trust.

After the Lebanon extraction I developed a reputation. When you've achieved something that nobody else has, you've instantly become a leading name in your field of work. Every company knows my name, or at least my alias.

Why you? How did you get into this line of work?

Honestly, this is the same answer that pretty much anyone can give to any question about their life. You don't sit around planning every little detail of your life. Things happen organically. Opportunities come up when you least expect them. It's serendipity, destiny, fate: you find yourself inexplicably drawn into something new.

The details aren't that interesting. I'd been injured as a military contractor in Afghanistan, temporarily losing most of my hearing from the sounds of explosions and gunfire, and had been medically discharged. An acquaintance had been bugging me for ages to get involved with rescuing children, though I hadn't got a clue what the business was all about. It's a bit like the military contracting: I hadn't got much idea what that was either when I started it, but everything fell into place and it was the right place to be.

After the main incident in this book – Lebanon - I got a name for myself. Every company knows my name, because I did something that nobody else has ever been able to do. People get in touch with me specifically to help them. They've tried traditional methods, often feeling completely let down by the system. When the government's website on international child abduction contains not-particularly-helpful suggestions like "try to come to an agreement with the other parent", you know they haven't got a clue.

People who contact me are looking for somebody to take them seriously, to investigate properly. The situation has deteriorated beyond the point of negotiation. The other parent is ignoring a court order. What's needed is a door-kicker who will chase leads, ask questions, take names and get results. Don't misunderstand me, it's not aggressive. *This is brains not brawn, mental ability rather than brute force.*

Chapter 3 - Growing Pains

"I'm afraid of not unlearning the bad things my parents taught me" - Trista Mateer

Don't expect me to talk in great detail about my childhood. I can't remember much of it. Before starting to write this book, I'd hidden those memories away in the deepest recesses of my mind. I still only remember small snippets, little snapshots of one memory or another.

My mum left when I was 2 years old, having been kicked out of the house by my dad after he learned that she'd been having an affair. Clear as day, I remember the last time that I saw her as a child. It was Mother's Day, the first one after she'd been thrown out of the house. I'd made her a card at nursery school, and remember my childlike feeling of excitement that I would finally be allowed to see her and give her the card. She came to the door. I was sitting on the stairs next to the door, but soon she and my father started arguing. It all happened in front of me: my mother trying to push her way into the house to see us, and my father pushing in the opposite direction to shut the door on her. From that day on, I wouldn't see her again until I was 16 when I finally 'met' her properly.

Throughout my childhood, she seemed to show no real interest in us at all. That's often how things are with alcoholics. It's very sad, but that's just the way life is. There was always some excuse to explain why she couldn't meet us, or at least that's how our dad made it sound. Looking back now, with the benefit of hindsight, it's difficult to know what to believe or how to make sense of it all. There were times when my father dropped us off outside the flats to meet up with her, and we'd sit there waiting for hours for her to turn up – but she never did. My dad would come back hours later, picking us back up. I have so many unanswered questions about my mum, things which don't seem to add up however I look at them.

My dad was a violent man. He wasn't particularly pleased to have been left in charge of me, or of my older brother and sister, and he showed his displeasure by doling out regular beatings.

Little memories float into my head. There's the time when, aged around 10 or 11, I remember my father putting a knife to my throat. I pushed the knife away, making my fingers bleed in the process. He threatened to cut them off. There's the time when he tried to ram a weights bar into my head. I certainly received plenty of beatings. I could handle them. But then, growing up in that environment, I suppose that anyone would learn to take them. There wasn't exactly any choice in the matter.

My brother quickly learned how we communicated in the family, often waking me up by hitting me because I was breathing too loudly for him. I had a bit of a better relationship with my big sister, though we drifted out of contact for a while when she was in her twenties whilst she was in an abusive relationship and struggling with depression. Of anyone, she's the only one of my close family that I still have any kind of relationship with today.

My brother wasn't the only one who'd learned all about violence. I rapidly became fluent in the very same language, often getting in trouble for using my fists in a street fight. From the age of 9, my mind was made up about my future career path. I knew that I was going to join the Army and fight. It would be the best decision I'd ever make: in the Army, for the first time in my life I would have people around me that I could rely on.

There's only really one big childhood memory that I haven't repressed. My dad took us on holiday to a caravan park down in Devon with his new girlfriend. It was the only holiday I ever went on as a child, but that's not the reason that it was memorable. I would have been 12 or maybe 13 at the time, developing the seemingly obligatory pubescent boy's keen interest in the opposite sex. I started chatting up some girl on the caravan site, who would end up becoming a pen pal later.

Apparently my dad went to the bar. What followed didn't make any sense to me, and I never understood this particular beating until I actually got round to confronting my dad about it some years later when I was safely out of the house. From what I gather, he was sitting in the bar and two guys saw me on the CCTV cameras playing pool with my new crush, having a good laugh and talking to her. It turns out that they were making a bet on whether I'd get the phone number or not. As a parent I know if my boy was doing that, I'd be on his side backing him 100%, cheering him on. Not my father: he was betting against me. I don't know quite why he was so embarrassed or why he caused a commotion, but when I had some measure of success getting the girl, he came right out and blamed me for embarrassing him. On the way back to the caravan, he proceeded to batter the living fuck out of me.

I can take a punch. Growing up in a violent family teaches you that. Something was different this time though. I disappeared, running off the site. I tried to get myself out of the situation, never having seen him quite this angry before. I didn't dare think about what he would do if I'd gone back to the caravan. After a while, a pair of car headlights appeared on the road behind me as I was walking down to the beach. The car wasn't being driven by my dad. It was a couple of older youths, maybe 18 or 19 or so. My hairs stood on end, that undefinable sixth sense warning me of impending danger. I could tell that much. I was in the Army cadets and also street smart. I knew the car was following me, and I also knew better than to head down an alleyway in the dark. An alleyway is no place to be caught by people who wish you harm. Instead, I jumped over a fence, knowing that a car couldn't possibly follow me. I headed out to another main road, only to find that the same car was there once more – still following me. I tried to memorise the registration plate, darted into a phone box and called the police. I must have got a letter or number wrong because they said that the plate didn't exist.

I moved on, spotting two people at the bus stop. I asked them to help me because this car was following me. As they started talking to the occupants of the car, I realised "fuck it's their friends". I started running again. Into people's gardens, trying to manoeuvre my way back. I saw the car again and darted out of the way. I also saw a police car go by, blue lights flashing, heading down in the general direction of the phone box I'd called them from. Perhaps they'd taken my call seriously, or maybe it was just coincidence. I don't know, because there was no way I was sticking around to satisfy my curiosity. Finally, I found my way back to the caravan site. I still couldn't go back into the caravan, fearing further rage from my dad, so I ended up sleeping in one of those traditional old red phone boxes which were still in regular use on the site, in the days before mobile phones rendered them obsolete and turned them all into overpriced rip-off ATM machines. Nobody came looking to work out where I was. Nobody gave a fuck. The next day though, everyone just acted like nothing had happened. I guess my dad didn't bear grudges. If he had one redeeming feature, maybe that was it.

Until recently, I didn't fully understand why – psychologically – I have such a passion for my work in child recovery. I mean yes, of course I love the fucking thrill of it. The adrenaline, the chase, all of that has been part of my psyche since I was a kid. I could say the same thing about the Army, private military contracting or maritime security, but to me there's a different emotional connection. They were jobs, but child recovery is a vocation.

I was chatting to a producer about making my life story into a film, telling him that I wasn't sure why exactly I do what I do. He said that it's obvious from my childhood. It's a connection within my subconscious, a strong innate desire. It pushes me towards doing this child recovery business. That's what makes me so passionate about it. The fact that I'm ex-military, and that I'm used to seeing action in private military contracting, just means that I've got the right physical and mental toolkit to be good at the job.

Sixteen years and nine months. That's how old you have to be to join the British Army. That number was etched into my mind. I'd known since primary school that I wanted to go to war. I can't explain why, but the Army green was coursing through my veins. When I was 12, I lied about my age to join the Army Cadets. I had a talent for marksmanship, so it wasn't long before I was on the Cadets' shooting team. By the age of 14, I was shooting for the county at Bisley.

Careers advisers had kept telling me that I needed another option, that I couldn't be so focused on just one potential job. If I didn't get into the Army, what was I going to do instead? They insisted that I would need some kind of education and ability to learn a trade. "Don't worry about it", I would say. I had zero doubt in my mind that I was going to make it. It was their job to try to get me to think about alternative options, but I just wasn't interested.

At 15 I'd just about had enough of waiting. I was a boy on a mission, so I had no desire to wait any longer than necessary to sign up. I decided to try and get into the Army anyway. I don't know if I was planning to lie about my age like I'd done to get into the Cadets, but I skipped school for the day and headed down to the Army Careers Office to try to join the Marines. At that young age I didn't have much idea about the Marines. I didn't know they were any different from the infantry. I was just the kind of kid who thought that the Army are soldiers, the Navy is all submarines, and the air force just flies around dropping bombs on stuff. My knowledge was a bit sketchy, to the point that I didn't even know what I was trying to join.

The recruiting officer, on the other hand, wasn't a total fucking idiot. He wouldn't exactly have needed to be Sherlock Holmes to deduce that I wasn't old enough to be there. It must have been clear as day to him that I was skiving school, but he humoured me anyway. He asked me to do some pullups, which I couldn't do. It was like a proper kick up the arse. It wasn't just that I was a little away from what was required. I hadn't got the first idea of the Army's requirements. The recruiting officer showed me the massive gulf between my standard of fitness and the standard required to join the Army. He suggested that I should go back to school and do some serious work on my fitness, then come back when I was old enough. He was nice enough – as a recruiting officer, he's paid to be. He's just like every salesman ever: paid to be nice, offer false promises and cuddly lies designed to get people to sign their lives away with the stroke of a pen.

I left school the moment that I could, taking a job working in a factory. Now I knew that my physical fitness needed to improve dramatically,

I would make sure to train every day. I'd run to work and run home again afterwards. I was glad to be earning, but not quite so glad as my dad. He wasn't so bothered about me leaving school but his eyes lit up at the sight of the money I was bringing in, which he took great pleasure in extracting from me and keeping for himself.

Meanwhile, I was ticking the days off on my mental calendar, looking forward to the day I could join the Army with my dad's permission. He certainly wasn't afraid to sign those papers because it meant he could get rid of me.

I arrived at Winchester railway station, the meeting point from where I would be taken to the Sir John Moore Barracks for Phase 1 of my basic training. There was a recruiting officer standing there. There were thirty or so of us raw recruits, all confused, none of us knowing what was going on or each other. Here we go, I thought. This is it. The confusion was probably all part of the plan. Not knowing what to do, you'd follow suit. Subtly, subconsciously, we were being conditioned to the Army way. When in doubt you fall in, and do what everyone else is doing. I filled in the necessary paperwork, signing away the next few years of my life, and was ushered on to a typical Army green 4-tonne truck to my way across to the barracks.

They say that joining the Army is supposed to be a bit of a culture shock for most people, but it had very little impact on me in that way. I was already accustomed to sharing a room with someone much less pleasant than my future Army mates, and even the discipline wasn't that new because I was always getting fucking knocked around at home anyway. I'm sure a lot of the others were shocked by the rough-and-ready 1990s attitudes to training, but it didn't make much difference to me. We always used to say "it doesn't matter what they do, they can't make you pregnant". I guess that phrase has probably dropped out of use, given that the gender balance in the Army is a bit more diverse than it once was.

I had no problem obeying orders: growing up with my dad, I'd already received compulsory basic training in being told what to do and not asking any questions because I'd get fucking hit if I opened my mouth anyway. When they say "jump", you don't even ask how high. You jump first and ask questions later, or preferably not at all. They don't like being questioned. On a military operation there won't be time for questions.

Because I'd been in the Cadets I was familiar with the weapons, the fieldcraft and the tactics on the ground. As a soldier, they go further. They teach you to be a professional, taking you to the next level of military understanding. Having a basic understanding already from the Cadets made a big difference though, standing me in good stead to be able to pick everything up quickly. This was nothing like school; I excelled in this environment – and I loved it!

The Army used to destroy your character, tearing apart everything about you. They would push you to your limits, and nothing you ever did would ever quite meet the standards they were looking for. Even if you were the perfect soldier, having spent hours polishing your boots ready for parade so that they were glistening in the midday sun, some drill sergeant would decide that they were scuffed, mess them up and make you start again. If your locker was absolutely pristine, they'd still find fault with the tidiness and throw your stuff out of the window to be collected later. Basic training was intense: never a moment to spare, a hundred-mile-an-hour lifestyle where every minute of your day was already planned out for you in great detail. It was 11 weeks of gruelling hell, breaking us physically and spiritually in the process. Breaking us, though, was the point.

It's all part of the process of rebuilding you into the Army's mould: to make you into that confident, authoritative person able to fit into the command structure – equally at home with giving or receiving orders, working within a team as a consummate professional. They had to break you first to rebuild you. Don't get me wrong, I'm glad that I joined the Army. It made me the man I am today. That's where my life really began. If you've ever seen that advert "I was born in Blyth, but I was made in the Royal Navy", it's more than just an enticement to join. It's true. Join the Armed Forces, and they'll make you.

You'll be made according to the same mould as every other soldier, of course. In order to do that they have to demoralise you, make you into an empty zombie-like shell, to rebuild you into a better person, one who's more useful to your country. Not everyone can hack it: of the thirty recruits who joined at the same time as I did, just thirteen of us remained on the parade square by the time we were done with basic training.

The whole thing is very controlled, with a hint of brainwashing behind it. You become institutionalised. It's eerily quiet when you go to sleep on your own, without your colleagues sharing your barracks. Many soldiers would leave the Army not knowing even the basics of how to live a civilian life. Some of us had never paid an electricity bill, developed basic computer skills, or cooked a family-style meal. That's one of the reasons why so many former squaddies end up living rough, falling into addiction or a life of crime, and why hundreds of Army veterans commit suicide every year. They'd try to keep people from quitting, telling us that without civilian qualifications there was nothing outside the Army for us – that we'd end up working in McDonalds. They'd tell us whatever they could to keep us.

We were taught not to ask too many questions. Wars are fought by young men because they're fit, but also because they're fearless and ruthless. Older, wiser men question things, asking why. But it wasn't until I got out of the Army, and spent time with some old-fashioned gnarled and seasoned veteran mercenaries, fashioned in conflicts from continent to continent, before I would even begin to understand that.

Don't get me wrong, I'm absolutely glad that I had the Army experience and it helped me no end. It's not all a perfect life though. There's good and bad about it, positives and negatives like any other way of life. I served on active duty in Northern Ireland, Kosovo and Sierra Leone. The tours in Jordan, Falklands and Gibraltar were non-operational, in the same way as a nineteenth century soldier might easily have been offered a cushy garrison duty I suppose. Honestly, though, that wasn't for me. I crave the adrenaline. I crave the action. I crave anything but sitting around doing nothing, bored out of my skull. Eventually, I headed out to Iraq. That was the first time I saw any real action, but in fact there was nothing worthy of the name – nothing which would truly compare to what I saw when I became a private military contractor.

The trigger for me to finally take the decision to leave the Army was a Ukrainian woman who I'd met, living in Italy. Up to that point, I'd just assumed that everyone would look favourably upon members of Her Majesty's Armed Forces. She had a different take on it. In Eastern Europe, they actually look down on their soldiers because that's all they can do. Sure, they can hold a gun but they're basically uneducated cannon fodder, mindless automatons who are programmed to blindly follow orders. In my experience, most of them were indeed useless – but to be fair I've met some real gems too: good, decent, hard-working soldiers.

I started to develop a desire for more money, better jobs, and I wanted to experience a luxury that I'd never had in life: not having people screaming over me every five minutes. I can't say that I knew what I wanted to put in its place. Frankly I didn't have a clue about that. I just knew that it was time to move on. Moving on didn't mean the Ukrainian woman: she was the type to just shag everything she saw.

I headed home, sleeping on my uncle's couch in Wolverhampton for a while. I didn't particularly feel like sticking around: the whole drinking culture wasn't what I wanted to be around, so I headed back to my home town. I found myself sleeping on the streets, but also at that time a goal crystallised in my mind. I wanted to earn a 6-figure salary. It's the first time that I ever became aware, in any sense, of the 'law of attraction'. I visualised my goal, and then life seemed to work out in such a way as to make it happen. I was using computers in the local library to check my emails. My colour serjeant contacted me, asking how I was getting on. I was honest: nothing at all was happening, I was sleeping rough, and I was searching for something to do. He sent me a link back to thirteen different military contracting companies working out in Iraq.

Surprisingly, I had absolutely no idea what these companies actually did. When I'd been out in Iraq with the Army, a civilian British guy had come to the barracks. His journalist client had been kidnapped. It's bad enough losing any client, but he'd gone and managed to lose the one client who could have him plastered all over the front page of the newspapers. An operation was swiftly launched to find the client.

It was an interesting operation, and an enjoyable one apart from the result, but it was a complete fucking shambles. The guy came up to the gate, totally shaken up, telling me that his client had been kidnapped. I was in the Ops room at the time, so I went down and brought him in.

All we needed to do was act quickly, and we might well have got to them in time. But we didn't. It took us from mid-afternoon until 6am the next morning before the cogs in the wheels of Army bureaucracy finally started to turn. It was so slow and long-winded.

Even when we got to the staging point, we larked around in that area for a good few hours. It felt as though we were on holiday and shit. We got the location for the house, and our orders were finally to stay around it and surround it. 22 SAS, the Hereford lot, were told to come down and join us. My job was to be the signaller, and we were ordered to wait for dawn. Even when someone took a pot shot at us, we didn't even respond to that. By the time we slowly crawled in at some point later that morning, everyone had already bugged out. That's what happens when you use ancient tactics in a modern war. It couldn't have been much worse if we'd got a trebuchet and started throwing fucking rocks at them.

By the time we finally got in there was nothing remaining but the body armour and helmet of the client. There was a blue helmet and body armour. The two SAS guys, in jeans and t-shirts, walked in and threw some shit around. They realised that there wasn't anything that they could do and fucked straight off. The entire operation had taken over 14 hours to press the button and move. Fourteen fucking hours in a time-sensitive operation that needed to be launched in fourteen minutes.

If I sound angry, it's because it was just such a senseless waste. I don't even know the journalist's name. I can't look him up, or try to find out what had happened to him. I haven't a clue. I've questioned it quite a lot over the years, wondering. There's a possibility that he's still alive. This happened well before the time they started chopping off heads. That didn't happen until 2004. He could have been murdered, yes, but it's equally likely that he could have been used as a pawn in a ransom or an exchange. That's the thing about the Army. You're not paid to think, you're paid to follow orders. You don't always find out what happened. You do your job, and that's that.

The whole experience was pretty baffling to me. It's not just that I didn't know much about the private contracting industry, I actually didn't have any more of a clue about what it was than House had about how to work in child recovery.

All I knew, and I only knew that from my colour serjeant, was that these companies were working in Iraq. Whilst I'd been living down and out, I'd been pretty down and borderline-suicidal. The only thing I knew how to do was soldiering. The danger didn't bother me. When I was offered a job, particularly for the money, I jumped at the chance. I went from being homeless to having a six-figure job in under a week. I lived like a soldier, so I'd die like a soldier. I would become a hired gun, a mercenary, playing Russian roulette with my life and being paid handsomely for it. Most of the private contractors, at least the Brits, hate that word. They don't want to be described as mercenaries, feeling that in a sense it's demeaning. They want to build a reputation as being professionals, providing security services. I get that, at least to an extent. It's also perfectly true to point out the blindingly obvious. We were still working for a foreign government, getting paid in U.S. dollars and doing things that U.S. soldiers should be doing. As much as people in my line of work think it's something like a joke shop to call ourselves mercenaries, in essence it is what we are.

I excelled at the work. It suited me so well, and I learned the job very quickly under the guidance of some seasoned veterans. There were South African old-school mercenaries, the last of their generation. They, on the other hand, used the word mercenary as something of a badge of honour – a word they could be proud of, not terrified of using. This was like the United Nations of soldiering: Americans, British, Polish, Nepalese, and (worryingly at the time) both Bosnian and Serbian. Some of them were in their forties, fifties and sixties. I'm pretty sure that at least one was seventy. There were Vietnam vets, and people who'd been part of pretty much any African coup in the last twenty years. Warfare was their lifestyle, the only thing they had truly learned in life, but they'd learned it well. The evidence that they were good at what they did was plain for all to see: they'd put their bodies on the line so many times, and were alive to tell the tale, having a very reasonable expectation of being paid handsomely for the job they did.

The South Africans especially taught me something new. They taught me how to control my anger and how to channel it into something positive. They taught me how to think independently, nurturing and developing my ability to plan operationally without the command structure umbrella that was part and parcel of Army life. At the age of 22 I was the youngest contractor out in Iraq – I was even mentioned in a PBS documentary for that reason. In the Army, I'd learned how to soldier. In the contracting business, I learned how to plan operations for myself. They took what the military did and brought me on to a different level. They'd play me some of the old South African war songs from the bush wars whilst we were having a braai (South African barbecue, much better than ours). They were proper tunes. It was a lifestyle to me, the way I wanted to be at that time, with a hard core of patriotism behind it.

Hearing their pride in their country stirred something inside me: a shared bond of patriotism despite coming from different hemispheres and cultures, the songs moving and motivating me too. I love my country but that doesn't mean I love everything it does. I love my country, but that doesn't mean I hate anyone else's. I love my country, but that didn't stop me living in Cyprus for two decades and developing a warm feeling towards Cypriot people and culture. Patriotism is a strange thing, but in its purely positive form in my experience it unites us and doesn't divide us. I've worked with Americans over the years, being very close to many of them, so I have almost a worldly sense of patriotism: yes it's British first and foremost, but it's also Cypriot, American and South African.

I was absolutely convinced that I was going to die in Baghdad. There was a sense of morbid mortality that followed me. It was a dangerous job. That's why they pay the big money, because your life expectancy doing a job like that is pretty short. You're expendable. They can always pay someone else a six-figure salary, but they can't replace a client who's just been blown to pieces. The person you're protecting is more important than you are. If you put your life above theirs, you're not going to last five minutes working in that industry.

When I went out to Iraq, I wasn't just resigned to dying. In a way, I almost welcomed the possibility. I'd find myself taking risks without really caring about my own safety. My mindset started to mellow as I got to know some of the people out there, gradually learning that life could have positives along with the negatives. There was a camaraderie, plenty of banter and laughs, and some strange, indescribable sense of belonging. My attitude slowly changed. Now I knew that death would likely happen to me at some point whilst I was out there, but it was no longer something I wanted. I was more indifferent to it. *If it happens, it happens.* That's the nature of the lifestyle: it's a risk of death every time you get into that vehicle and drive out of those gates. I suppose, though, that not caring if I lived or died was progress. Better than wanting to be dead.

Chapter 4 -
The price of life

"How much is a human life worth? Individuals, families, companies, and governments routinely place a price on human life. The calculations that underlie these price tags are often buried in technical language, yet they influence our economy, laws, behaviours, policies, health, and safety." - Howard Steven Friedman

Route Irish was the most dangerous road in the world, used as a training ground for Al Qaeda terrorists. It's a seven and a half mile stretch of hell, linking Baghdad's Green Zone to its international airport. Many of the locals would refuse to go anywhere near it. Good luck to anyone at that time wanting to get a taxi willing to risk taking you to the airport.

There were explosives going off everywhere, craters in the road and constant debris to avoid whilst driving. Every hole caused by an explosion was given only the quickest of repairs: nobody wanted to hang around a second longer than they had to. Imagine losing your life because you spent a few seconds too long fixing a pothole in the road – hardly the most glamorous way to go out. The road was a death trap, literally.

People used to say that our high-speed tactical driving meant private military contractors were a bunch of cowboys. They couldn't have been more wrong. Our tactics were dictated by the nature of our situation. Our high-speed driving had a genuine tactical reason. When an improvised explosive device (IED) goes off, your momentum is going to keep you moving forward and away from the people who are trying to kill you. The vehicle behind, following closely, is often effectively ramming you – forcing you to keep going, keeping you out of the way of danger. When we veered from side to side going under bridges, it was a simple defence mechanism. Suppose that someone at the top of the bridge, who you can't see, throws a grenade. They're not expecting you to switch lanes. In the time it takes for that grenade to land, you're no longer in its path. The tactics changed, in the end, because the level of risk changed. There would eventually come a point, a crossover, when the road was sufficiently safe that such tactics were more likely to result in a road traffic accident than to save your life. At that time, tactics changed. That's what military strategy is all about: achieving your objectives whilst minimising loss of life. When the situation changes, so do your tactics.

Terrorists were trained on Route Irish precisely because they knew there was the largest concentration of Westerners anywhere in Iraq. Think about it for a moment. It's absolutely obvious that if there's a major road connecting the capital city to its main airport, you're going to have a lot of traffic desperate to go down that route. The United States also had a military base at the airport, having converted Saddam Hussein's former palaces both there and in the Green Zone.

Route Irish was brutal. Terrorists would place IEDs inside dead dogs on the side of the road, with the idea that nobody would be anticipating a dog being blown to smithereens and taking them with it. On one occasion, which I found particularly disgusting, they even implanted explosives inside a live donkey and detonated that. It was sick. War is vicious, horrible and bloody – but even war has rules. Terrorists didn't have those. Whatever they could do to kill and maim was good enough for them.

I learned to drive on Route Irish. I don't just mean that figuratively. I mean it literally: I didn't yet have a licence, but the usual rules didn't apply to war-torn Iraq. I'd be driving at up to 140mph. I learned to change a tyre under fire on the same route. This is the stuff that would take many hours to teach you in a classroom, but you'll learn it in minutes in the middle of action when your life is on the line.

Survive Route Irish and you can survive anything.

We're a three-vehicle convoy heading down Route Irish, protecting our client. Our client is in the middle vehicle, which means that the front and rear vehicles are both expendable. We want to present a moving target. In war-torn Iraq, you don't exactly have to worry about picking up a speeding ticket. The safest speed to drive is over 100 miles per hour. That makes you a moving target. By the time an enemy insurgent or suicide bomber realises that you're in the area and tries to form an ambush, you're too far away for them to do anything. We'd take vehicles on the ranges, doing real-life training. We would simulate attacks at high speeds. Nobody was fucking around. Get it wrong and you'd be dead, your mates would be dead – and more importantly, your client would be dead.

We hit heavy traffic in front. Traffic jams are always a problem on Route Irish. They turn you from a moving target into a stationary one. Not good. There's only one thing for it: we cross the central reservation and speed down the opposite side of the road into oncoming traffic. If that sounds reckless, remember that the lead vehicle is expendable. Every single movement we made was dangerous in the eyes of a normal civilian, but it was all tactical, designed to minimise risk.

The locals know this can happen. They don't want to be in the fast lane unless they absolutely have to be. They know to stay away. We spot a military callsign: three U.S. military vehicles. Just a single look is enough for us to know that's the cause of the traffic jam: they're intentionally holding traffic back away from them to ensure that they were protected. We'd have done exactly the same thing, it just happened to be inconvenient for us on that day. They're static and have guns trained on two civilian vehicles, pointing and waving them away. Unfortunately, they're being waved onto our side of the road.

Suicide bombers. That's most likely what the U.S. military vehicles are trying to avoid. And now, we've just become a pretty appealing target. You see, American military are Westerners. But we're Westerners too. Our client is a Westerner. If bombers can't blow up a U.S. military vehicle, they're equally happy to blow us up. They just like blowing up Westerners really. It's what they do. This was war against Al Qaeda. All Western forces and NGOs were at risk, 24 hours a day.

The beheadings hadn't started yet. Ken Bigley was the first person to get his head cut off, having been kidnapped just a few streets away from us. I used to have nightmares about that, being captured and feeling like I was having a rusty knife stuck into my neck. I'd wake up, physically choking, whilst the other guys sharing my room would look at me weirdly.

I analyse my dreams all the time. Dreams, to me, are just your subconscious trying to find some way of processing everything that's gone on during the day. They contain subtle, coded messages. After a while, I started to understand the meaning of that particular dream. I needed to slow down. I was always trying to move too fast, looking to get myself promoted as quickly as I possibly could.

There would constantly be people coming in and out of the teams because of the level of danger. Some would die, others had made their money and decided to move on, and then there were the so-called 'ex-special forces' guys who just couldn't hack it. You could tell those Walter Mittys a mile off. They'd show off, flaunting SAS-type experiences and credentials as a badge of honour – but clearly they'd never been anywhere near real action. The moment the explosions started, they'd shit themselves and they'd be on the first plane home. And there was the total nutter who wanted to use Iraq as a way of learning how to kill so that he could go back home and kill everyone who was part of a cult he'd grown up in. They say 'there's always one', but that one really took the piss. Then there were the sackings: you'd be out on your ear within minutes if you'd made a serious mistake. If your life was expendable to the company, they certainly wouldn't have any qualms about firing you on the spot either.

Once I understood that I needed to stop being so ambitious and chasing promotions, the nightmares stopped. I needed to chill out. Promotions happened naturally because there were so many vacancies. Within four months I was the youngest 2IC (second in command); within seven, I was the youngest team leader.

Today I'm in the lead vehicle of the convoy, a big Ford Excursion SUV. They're an imminent threat. We've got signs up at the back instructing everyone to "stay back 100 metres". The sign's a bit optimistic, to be honest. Nobody's going to keep up with us. The reason was more to cover ourselves. If someone did manage to speed up at our rear, they'd know that they'd been warned not to come any further. Anyone coming towards us would be deemed as a threat instantly.

They could have every possible warning: we had the 'blues and twos' to use when needed. If they ignored the flashing lights, horns and sirens – well then, there was no surprise if something went wrong. We got into a bit of trouble with the United States because we called our rear vehicle the "widow maker". It's the rear vehicle which was most likely to find itself doing any shooting. We had a pirate flag and "widow maker" on the back. To us it was just a bit of a laugh, but when it ended up in the Washington Post the U.S. Government got in touch with us. They explained very simply that we needed to take that down straight away. It wasn't very good for their 'hearts and minds' policy in

Iraq, to say the least.

They're coming right for us. The rules of engagement (which would later be renamed as the Rules for the Use of Force – and rebranded to say exactly the same thing in nice, friendly, fluffy language which was more acceptable to civilian bureaucrats) allow me to take a shot to disable the vehicle. To protect my client, I have no choice. I must do so. But our vehicle is armoured. I can't exactly wind the window down and fire from within it.

"Do. Not. Fucking. Move", I instruct my driver. I trust him with my life – in fact, I'm about to do exactly that. As we're zooming down the Iraqi highway at a hundred-plus miles per hour, the only viable option isn't very appealing. I open the door, getting down onto the running board step used to enter and exit the vehicle. To steady my gun, I wedge it between the door and the frame. Once it's secure, I have a steady shot - though doing so in the open air at that speed is somewhat challenging. This isn't exactly something that you practice in basic training. I take two shots into the engine block of the lead vehicle. It's enough to disable it, and the other vehicle backs off.

Now there's another problem: how to get back into the vehicle and get the door closed once I've finally managed to get my gun out of the awkward position it's now wedged in. Fortunately, my driver knows exactly what to do. He makes the right call and swerves the vehicle suddenly. The door slams shut, and I'm thrown across the car – knocking my head right into his crotch.

"Yeah, um, whilst you're down there mate..."

It's a quirky kind of humour. There's no possibility of anyone being offended: when you're risking being blown to bits by an improvised explosive device at any second, you're hardly going to be the kind of sensitive soul to take offence at a slightly sexualised joke. That's the humour that gets you through the day, the light relief so that everything doesn't seem too morbid.

Shit, I think. Something's dropped out of my pocket – or has it? I'm not sure, the sounds are being eclipsed by everything else that's going on. I hope not, but then the vehicles behind open radio communications to tell me that something's dropped from our vehicle.

What have I lost? My first thought is that it's my pistol or magazine. That's a big no-no. The last thing you want is to be accidentally handing weapons and ammunition to the enemy. Imagine the irony of getting killed by your own weapon because you were too much of an idiot to keep hold of it – that would be the ultimate humiliation. Losing a weapon would be a sacking offence for the company, and even if they didn't sack you there'd be a permanent mark against your name, but that's not as bad as doing the same in the military. Lose your weapon and you'd be headed off to military jail. Believe me, the stories I've heard about the glasshouse would make a regular prison seem like an absolute holiday camp.

We'd never be able to go back and fetch anything. Route Irish is far too dangerous for anything like that. Whatever has gone is gone for good. My heart drops, with a feeling of impending doom as I start to check my kit. I'm puzzled for a moment: there's nothing actually missing. It doesn't make sense until I grab a cigarette. I reach for my Zippo, and it's not there. I have to laugh: I'd literally bought a new one an hour before, and it's still sitting there in a shopping bag in the back seat. Such an irony, just another strange example of how the universe works.

My decision to take those actions in support of American soldiers was a spontaneous one, but it led to a commendation from a two-star U.S. General. Their Command Sergeant Major shook my hand and gave me a commemorative coin as though it were a medal, thanking me for my quick thinking and helping him out. "That", he told me, "was the ballsiest move I've ever seen". I'll never forget that day because I was acting all cool, fobbing it off with a that's-how-we-roll kind of attitude. The Americans use the g-spelling of Sergeant, which still doesn't sit easily with me as a former light infantryman. We stuck to the traditional spelling Serjeant, which seems to have been lost in the mists of time but still retained by the rifles and other light infantry regiments in the United Kingdom. The next week, I navigated a convoy through a mortar attack. This time, the rest of my team also got the coin. Two such acts within the space of a week attracted the attention of the top brass, and I was put forward for a commendation by General Bostock.

Truthfully, though, there was not much special about it: the level of danger I was facing on a daily basis was simply par for the course. If anything, the only thing to single those incidents out from hundreds or thousands of others happening in Iraq on a daily basis was the fact that the incidents happened to occur right in front of the nose of American military officers. They were grateful, and we were just doing our job. That's the private military contracting business: soldiers for hire, all the bravery you need for one low, low price of just 11 grand a month.

Chapter 5 -
The privatisation of death

"Peace is purchased in the currency of loss" -
Glen Duncan

The American government had a problem. The war in Iraq was remote, a long way from home, and the public was hardly convinced of the need to be there in the first place. As the bodies started to pile up, coffins flown back draped in the American flag, people were starting to protest. They didn't understand why their brothers, husbands, fathers or sons were dying in some far-off land that they couldn't locate on a map.

Private military contracting was the answer. The American government took all the tasks which weren't specifically soldiering, and outsourced them to private companies. These were usually the most dangerous tasks, so the deaths moved away from official statistics and into the hands of private companies. In a very real way, the U.S. had just privatised death.

Saddam Hussein's palaces were in Baghdad. Some were in the Green Zone, but the majority were at Camp Victory at the airport. The American military commandeered them, using them as military bases. I got to know the palace which had belonged to Uday Hussein, the Ace of Hearts in the playing cards deck of "most-wanted Iraqis" made by the U.S. Defense Intelligence Agency. The palace had been turned into a U.S. military MWR building – which means morale, welfare and recreation. It's their equivalent of the British Naafi (Navy, Army and Air Force Institute) building: somewhere soldiers can go for some downtime, play pool and generally escape from the stresses of war. If you need help and support, that's where you go. That building also doubled as a waiting area for contractors. If we were picking up of dropping off a client, and it didn't really matter whether the client was civilian or military because everything was strangle intermingled, that's where we would wait. The U.S. military used to give out free "Rip-it" drinks, which was the American equivalent of drinking a

Monster or Red Bull. Every soldier and contractor used to live off Rip-its, at least until 2015 when the U.S. military did a quick about-turn and banned them because each serving contains something like 4,000% of your recommended lifetime caffeine intake (according to then U.S. Army Surgeon General Cal Ripkin).

This building had a grim and chequered history – Uday Hussein hadn't become the 'Ace of Hearts' without a reason. However bad the media made Uday Hussein sound, the truth was far worse. Our car park was converted from a lion pit which had housed alligators, lions and other animals during Saddam's reign of terror. Uday was a power-hungry bully, the type who would use the dictatorial power which came to him nepotistically from his father.

He was a rapist, a paedophile and a murderer. He would have girls and women brought to his palace, or simply take them from the streets. There were grim, sick rules behind his womanising – he'd never sleep with the same woman three times. He preferred not to forcibly rape them, but it was well known what happened to girls who didn't willingly agree to sleep with him, so most of them did what they were told. He had a thing for having girls brutally flogged, often on the soles of their feet.

I learned much of Uday's history from the American soldiers I met there. Uday used to pick women up off the street, kidnapping them and taking them back to the palace. He'd either persuade them to sleep with him, or rape and torture them. It's said that he had a medieval torture device, the so-called 'Iron Maiden' – an iron case with metal spikes on the inside, in which he'd put those who displeased him. He treated athletes in the same way as he treated women, often torturing them and having them flogged for poor sporting performances.

The worst thing, though, was the way he treated those unfortunate souls who he would never let go. Survivors of Uday Hussein were starting to talk, so he decided not to leave so many survivors. The girls he kidnapped from the streets and took back to the palace would be raped and tortured. Then, as everyone stood there laughing and jeering, the terrified women would be thrown to the lions as though it were some ancient Roman amphitheatre. The lions became so accustomed to eating human flesh that they had to bring South African zookeepers in to get the lions back to a more acceptable diet and able to transport them out of there. The site of those killings became our car park; Uday Hussein's palace, our recreation room. Somehow, you could just feel it in your bones. The presence of evil was still there. It was palpable and horrible, sending shivers down the spine.

By November 2007, I'd just about had enough of being in Iraq. It was time for me to move on, and I was ready to leave just a few days later on December 3rd. Our local superstition was that it's a dangerous time. The people who died seemed to always be those who were just about to leave, or the ones who'd just had a new baby, or who were sent out on a mission on their birthday.

When I was attached to another team for a simple recce (reconnaissance mission) I didn't think too much of it. It was a straightforward mission, and I was just an extra shooter in the client vehicle. I was just tagging along to make up the numbers. Before the day was done, I'd be thinking about that superstition.

As you come out of the Green Zone, there's a turning which takes you up past an Iraqi checkpoint heading North. We'd had all sorts of minor shit there in the past, but thankfully no major incidents until now. As ever, for protection our vehicles were in a convoy. The Iraqi police commander waved the first vehicle through, then they stood in front of ours. That was the red flag moment in our minds. Now in 2007, our tactics were clearly known to Iraqi police. They'd know perfectly well that the second vehicle would most likely be the client vehicle. As it happens, this time there was no client being transported, but they didn't know that.

The rules, by this time, had changed. Iraqi police may have been dodgy as hell, and often connected to Al Qaeda, but technically they were allowed to stop us. They had never once attempted to do so before. The driver edged the vehicle forward. The situation didn't smell right: they were attempting to isolate one vehicle from the convoy. A while back, in Fallujah, contractors had been dragged out of a vehicle and lynched before setting it ablaze. Their dead, burned bodies were hung from a bridge over the river Euphrates. That incident had essentially caused the Battle of Fallujah, because the U.S. effectively turned round and said 'you're not doing that to our people'. It was a grisly fate, and we certainly didn't want the same thing to happen to us, so our driver put his foot on the accelerator pedal slowly. The Iraqi police commander was on the bonnet, but had no choice other than to let us go.

By the time we'd got to the top of the road though, they'd put a blockade in. We couldn't go through, and there was no way of turning off the road. Boxing off the road, to left and right, there were blast-proof reinforced concrete walls known as T-walls. Every so often, these walls would be buttressed by a thicker layer of concrete – making them look like an inverted letter T, hence the nickname T-walls. They were 12-foot high, reminiscent of the old Berlin Wall and giving an austere, cold, warlike impression.

We couldn't go forward, and we couldn't turn off, so there was only one remaining option: to go back. After a swift three-point turn, physically bouncing off the walls in our haste, the vehicle headed back down towards the same police checkpoint we'd just gone through. Get through that, and we'd be straight back into the Green Zone. The police commander stopped us again. There were four or five Iraqi police vehicles with PKMs (a Soviet general-purpose machine gun) mounted on the roof. They were strong enough to be able to penetrate our vehicle's armour without a doubt. The police had their mobile phones out, videoing us and sliding fingers across their throats as if to tell us "you're dead".

All our vehicles were now back together in the convoy, and locked. The Iraqis started trying to jimmy the doors open, whilst we were frantically pressing the transponder buttons to call the company and anyone else who'd listen to ask for help and backup. The company point-blank refused to offer us any assistance whatsoever. The game seemed to be up. We had no viable option, and were even contemplating the suicidal approach of making a run for it. The machine guns would have ripped our vehicles apart. Within minutes, we expected to be dragged out and either killed on the spot or fucking sold to Al Qaeda.

We were so alone, so isolated, and yet so close to base. The sense of betrayal, that the company was actively refusing to send us support, was terrifying. Our training had always been to press the emergency transponder button and open communications in the event that we ran into any difficulties. It was drilled into us, time and time again, that they were there to help. Yet the one time we actually needed some backup, what we heard was nothing but weakness and excuses.

I still don't know what happened. Were they concerned about sending more numbers out into a dangerous situation? Were they trying to negotiate for our release in the background? Were they trying to get us some military support? Those are the more charitable explanations.

The less charitable explanation is that we were simply expendable, and that it was a purely financial decision to let us die. After all, there was no client in our convoy. Our company might well have considered that it was worth sacrificing our lives to avoid the potential of a major incident which could potentially cost them the ability to get work in Iraq in the future.

Weak command? Sending out another vehicle with their numbers? Trying to negotiate in the background? I honestly don't know. The only thing we thought at the time is that we were on our own, just sitting there waiting.

Blackwater is the 'blue chip' company of private military contracting. Formed by ex-Navy SEAL Erik Prince, it's had fingers in pretty much every pie going. It's worked in every field from wars to hurricane relief, training people worldwide in security and warfare. They were of course a big presence in Iraq. Hearing the comms chatter on the radio, Blackwater offered us help. Our company refused the offer of assistance. There are what-the-fuck moments, and there are what-the-fuck moments. This was the biggest one of my life. Not sending resources to support us was bad enough, but actively stopping someone else from helping? Really?

Blackwater ignored them, and put snipers in the sky to support us anyway. We saw the little birds – bubble helicopters – in the sky. It gave us a moment of hope.

Another team of ours, coming back from its mission, heard the shit going down and radioed in to request permission to assist us. Once again, the offer of assistance was refused. We couldn't believe it, just minutes away from the doors being opened and certain death.

The team leader disobeyed orders. This wasn't the military, it was a private business operating in Iraq. They couldn't force him to let us die. He fucked the company right off, making it clear to his team what he was about to do, and let anyone who didn't have the stomach for the fight stay away. At this point they were perhaps 300 metres away, easy walking distance. They brought one vehicle with the doors open, and others on on foot with weapons and body armour. They walked past the American military checkpoint, picking up some U.S. soldiers on the way.

Shit was about to get real, and the bullets would fly if the situation wasn't de-escalated fast. It would be a bloodbath, but at least we might have some kind of fighting chance with ground reinforcements and aerial sniper support. The odds had been evened, which meant that at the very least we weren't going to be bullied any more.

It turned out that the bullets weren't going to be required. The Iraqi police might have opened fire on us, but opening fire on a U.S. soldier would be a whole different matter. That was a one-way ticket to an early grave and a repeat of the Battle of Fallujah. The soldier walked confidently up to the Iraqi police commander. Using a language my father would have understood, he let his fists do the talking and started punching the living daylights out of the Iraqi police commander. That gave us just the distraction we needed to fuck right off out of there. The lead vehicle gunned the throttle, ramming into the pick-up truck which was blocking us in, and we headed back to the Green Zone past the military checkpoint. That, we thought, would be the end of the matter. Apparently not. The team leader, whose heroic actions had saved our lives, was rewarded in typical military contracting fashion – by being sacked.

This wasn't 2003 Iraq, it was 2007. Our vehicles now had numbers: stickers attached to the door which acted as identifiers for each private military contracting company. The police could clearly determine which company we worked for. I was in the middle of a debrief on the car park when, within an hour or two of the incident, the mortar fire started. Now, I suppose it could be a complete coincidence that the worst mortar fire I ever experienced just happened to occur, concentrated around our base, straight after this happened. A more likely explanation would be that out of pure spite, the corrupt Iraqi police passed our details on to Al Qaeda terrorists who didn't exactly need a second invitation, or indeed a decent reason, to start shelling the fuck out of Westerners. I found myself riding a bicycle through the mortar attack, but that's another story.

Chapter 6 -
Piracy on the high seas

"A ship in harbour is safe, but that is not what ships are built for." - John A. Shedd

At around this time, in 2005, I met my future wife. I came back from Iraq on leave to Cyprus, and honestly my life was in a bit of a mess at the time. I was earning a six-figure annual salary, and every time I got leave I'd spend it in a five-star hotel: a bit of an upgrade from living on the streets just months earlier, a reminder of how lives can be transformed (or snuffed out) in the blink of an eye.

I'd date strippers, buy drinks for everyone in the bar, and generally party like a complete idiot. When off duty, my life was luxurious but cold. I didn't really have (or at least didn't admit to) any real emotions at the time. From the outside I was the life and soul of the party, but scratch the surface and there was a cold, almost detached, mentality lurking not too far beneath.

I'd never known a normal, loving family life. I wasn't used to a proper relationship. I'd often stay at work, not using up my leave. I'd give my leave away to other people. The war in Iraq was my lifestyle. After all, I felt comfortable in a life-or-death situation when I knew that my colleagues had got my back. I didn't feel the same way about a normal life back on civvy street.

When you're working on a PSD (protective security detail) for a private company in the middle of a war zone, you don't know whether you'll still be alive tomorrow. Even at night, you're running the risk of an ambush. You could fall asleep at night and be killed before you even have chance to wake up. You're living from minute to minute. The casualty rates are horrific, but of course that's why they pay you the eleven grand a month. It's the opposite of a highway robbery: instead of giving your money for your life, you give your life for your money.

This time though, I'd actually taken my leave because one of my best friends was due to get married. Perhaps it was the start of post-traumatic stress but I just wanted to be alone, craving some solitude. Ask any squaddie and they'll tell you all about Kokomo, a party bar in Cyprus. I headed for the quietest spot at around 4 in the afternoon, trying my best to avoid company. Yet when I had one idea, fate clearly had a different one. I honestly can't say that I had really noticed the lady serving my drinks. She'd seen me in the bar before with various women, thinking that I was just a player and a knobhead. The bar was quiet though, and I'm sure that she could sense something was up, so she came over and started talking to me.

Her eyes were sparking, an emerald green. That's the first thing I noticed, more so even than the fact that she was fit, skinny and wearing a short skirt. She had multiple colours in her long, thick hair – so many colours that you couldn't possibly tell what colour her natural hair actually was. I suppose I had already sort-of met her before: she'd served me at the bar multiple times in the past, but this was our first proper conversation.

I don't quite know how to describe it, but something inside me melted. There was a connection, a warmth. The more we spoke, the more I started to feel things. I'd never really felt anything for anyone before. Within a week we were engaged, and within a month we were married. If that sounds like it was ridiculously fast, try to understand that my life could have been ended at any moment. The life insurance at work wouldn't pay out if you weren't married, so there was a practical reason to hurry up. If I died, it would be far better for her to be provided for. The 8-week periods of intense duty, followed by usually 3 weeks of leave, added to the urgency. If we didn't get married quickly, it'd be another couple of months before I could see her again.

Like everything else in my high-octane lifestyle, I didn't have much patience for waiting around. We both knew that we wanted to get married, so we did. It was as simple as that.

It was a steep learning curve for me: I now had to learn how to become a human, more than anything. That caused all sorts of problems for me at the beginning of our marriage. I suddenly had to learn how to process my emotions, to avoid allowing myself to be controlled by them. Everything that had once been blocked off now came flooding out at once. Fortunately, my new wife was always there for me. I've grown immeasurably as a human being through knowing her.

Even so, getting married didn't change my fundamental approach to life – at least not at the start. I'd swung from one extreme to the other, going from wanting to die to feeling that I was somehow immortal because I'd survived so many close encounters. I'd take unnecessary risks, believing that I couldn't die. It honestly wasn't any healthier than when I'd wanted to die.

It took a long time, and the birth of my son, before I actually cared enough to want to protect my life in any way. If I died on duty, I knew that my wife would be provided for with the insurance package. At the time I didn't think so much about the emotional effect that my death would have on her, but more about her being financially secure. When my son was born, it was the shock that I needed. I didn't want him growing up without a dad. My own mortality was back, and now it had consequences. It would affect someone else.

Now that I truly understood I had a reason to live, I developed some superstitions. I hadn't been killed whilst wearing a pair of gloves, so I'd always wear the same pair of gloves when going out of the compound. If I'd forgotten them, I'd make the driver wait until I'd gone back to fetch them. I felt as though I'd got more purpose in life now, but I'm the kind of person to get bored very easily once I've learned as much as I can. After I'd been in Iraq for four and a half years, I immediately started asking "what's next on the agenda?"

Like everything else in life, the next move presented itself. Things just happen, at the right time, and in this case it turned out to be working in maritime security. The Gulf of Aden was a dangerous place towards the end of the noughties, with Somali pirates wreaking havoc on oil tankers and other vessels carrying lucrative cargo. I'd board a transit going from Egypt and the Red Sea, through the Suez Canal and the Gulf of Aden before heading down to Oman. Or I'd pick up in Djibouti, going to Dubai, Abu Dhabi or Yemen. I learned more about seamanship to go along with fieldcraft and marksmanship, something which would prove immeasurably more useful than I could have ever predicted later in life when it came to rescuing children.

Maritime was hell. I hated it. The food on the vessels was shit, and there was always some useless cunt in charge creating the rotation. Still, it was interesting. I was on the first Japanese military convoy outside Japanese waters since World War 2. In Japanese history, that was a momentous event: after the events of the 1930s and 1940s, there was a significant backlash in Japan against the use of the military. The Japanese Constitution specifically prohibits any aggressive military action or declaration of war: instead, its military is a "Self-Defence Force". In this case, of course, it was protection – but, hearing the choppers roar as aerial helicopter support patrolled our ships, it was certainly memorable to be part of this historic event.

Mostly, though, our missions were more Dad's Army than military powerhouse. Governments were slow on the uptake, slow to recognise the threats posed by Somali pirates and to understand the need to take action.

The sea is huge. You can't possibly patrol every square mile of it, and a ship in danger might not be able to expect rescuing Naval assistance for hours, or even longer. We were, to all intents and purposes, on our own. At the time – though thankfully it's changed now – laws would prohibit us from having the tools to do the job. Lacking an AK47, or even any kind of guns at all, we had to improvise. And improvise we did – with bastardised pyrotechnics: flares, chemicals and Molotov cocktails made with elastic bands. It was a Blue Peter approach to naval defence.

Somali pirates would jam our signals and push music through our radio comms to prevent us getting in touch with anyone from outside. On my first mission we got comms incoming from a French vessel that was being hijacked miles away. Surprisingly, I didn't really see much action whilst working at sea. Other vessels seemed to be attacked on a regular basis. The one time we were approached, the captain took control and was able to manoeuvre us back to safety.

The plan was firstly to prevent the ship from being boarded at all. In the event that we were boarded, we were prepared to lock the crew in the safe house (known as a 'citadel') of the engine bay and fight to retain control of the bridge for as long as we could. That wouldn't be easy if our hijackers had guns and we didn't, but we planned carefully. We'd throw hoses to knock off any boarders trying to use grappling irons to climb onto the ship, then if they managed to board there would be barricades on each stairwell. We'd be throwing Molotov cocktails down on them, and at every breach we'd retreat to repeat the process. Our tactic was to create defence after defence after defence, making it incredibly costly for even the most determined of attackers to capture the bridge and gain control of the ship. In the meantime, we'd be heading for the nearest port at top speed. Perhaps we wouldn't get there in time, and perhaps nobody would come to our aid, but at least we'd give ourselves the best possible chance. Of course, if we'd been allowed to have guns it would have been a fairer fight. Other vessels certainly got a lot of shit on those trips, but I didn't.

I started picking up other contracts in Guinea Bassau, Mali, and so on – but the best of all was working on the Prince of Abu Dhabi's yacht. It was an 85.2 metre yacht with a helipad and bars on board. On that vessel we were armed to the teeth: 50-calibre snipers, M4s and grenade launchers. The vessel's design, with a low deck on the back, made it difficult to protect but with the firepower we had, they wouldn't have stood a chance. We took on responsibility for training the team from the Royal Guard, teaching them to protect themselves. It was like being on board a floating 5-star hotel, and the food was absolutely amazing.

If that job had been permanent, I would have absolutely loved it. The money was indeed good, but it was all very seasonal. You'd get a few weeks taking the yacht from Abu Dhabi to Europe, then get off and let them crack on with whatever partying they had planned. In the autumn we'd do the return journey, or perhaps take it to the Maldives or for maintenance. But with only a few weeks at a time, sadly it was never going to be a long-term solution.

I ended up going out to Afghanistan. Honestly, I was really enjoying it: it was like working in Iraq all over again, but without one of the worst parts. Back in Iraq, they had EFPs – armour-piercing improvised explosive devices that could destroy you or a vehicle. In Afghanistan, that danger wasn't present. It was very much enjoyable until my injury.

The word "friendly fire" is an oxymoron. There's nothing friendly about being injured by one of your own side. Attacks happened in Afghanistan on a regular basis, and my work out there swiftly ended during one of them. The guy to my left simply got too close to me when discharging his weapon. I had an earpiece in my right ear, but nothing in my left. The sound was, literally, deafening. My eardrum retracted and I couldn't hear a thing out of that ear for another six months.

You might think that losing your hearing in one ear isn't that bad. Believe me, it is: every single sound feels like it's coming into your head at the same time, a jumbled cacophony of bizarre and irritating noises. I just had to cope with it. I was on medical leave with a workplace injury, being paid a percentage of my salary until I'd recovered for sitting around at home without having to risk my life. It was a particularly difficult time for my family though. I could be sitting with the TV on full blast trying to hear it, but one of my children would walk into the room and make only a small noise – and it'd be so painful because it set my bad ear off. I had to stop going into bars because the ambient noise would cause so much pain that I just couldn't cope with being there.

The company was required to hold my job open until I'd recovered, or to offer me an equivalent position instead. I was originally looking forward to getting back out there, but by the time I would have been healthy enough to return, something else had come up. Lebanon.

Chapter 7 - Ramshackle rescue

"By failing to prepare, you are preparing to fail"
- Benjamin Franklin

I'd known Daniel for years. I met him online, but for the life of me I couldn't remember where or how. We got on well enough, and I was quite happy to light-heartedly take the piss out of him for his somewhat unusual field, working in child recovery to rescue those who had been kidnapped and taken overseas. Secretly, though, it was something that I found intriguing. It was certainly a noble cause.

Every month he seemed to be getting in touch with me for something or other, asking me if I knew anyone that could help him out in the countries that he was working in. Whilst I was recovering from my injury, he was desperate for a 'fixer' and got in touch asking me if I could find him a point of contact in Lebanon. As fate would have it, I had just been working with a guy who was raised in Lebanon. Many things turn out to be about who you know rather than what you know, and my colleague was able to pass on the details of a guy he had grown up with. Six months' worth of court cases were fast-forwarded in just two weeks, but the basic problem was still the same.

Daniel wanted to meet up with me and get some fresh eyes on the job. It was troubling him. A Norwegian lady met her Lebanese partner in Australia (that's not the start of a joke or a riddle, of course) and gave birth to his baby daughter. All was going well, as far as she knew, until he took his girl on holiday. He never returned, having taken her to an area of Lebanon controlled by Hezbollah terrorists. It was an international abduction, with no chance of it being fully overturned by the Lebanese courts because Lebanon was not a signatory to the Hague Convention. Daniel's mission was to recover the child, but he was drawing a blank in terms of actually finding a plan to do it. The girl was now 4 years old, and everything seemed to be dragging slowly with no reasonable hope of anything being resolved in the near future. Her life, growing up in a Hezbollah-controlled town in

Northern Lebanon with a controlling father and Sharia system where women aren't permitted out of the house without being accompanied by a man, was unlikely to be a barrel of laughs if we couldn't get her out of there.

It was the first time I'd actually met Daniel, and he flew over to Cyprus specially. We met up, had a few beers, and he could see that I knew my shit. He called his boss Mick and set up a meeting. If I'm honest, I thought Mick was a bit of a knobhead. It wasn't just that this short bald Norwegian ex-paramedic seemed to think he was the boss of a large private army, parading himself around as though he owned the world itself. The worst part was that his supreme arrogance, talking down to everyone around him, was exceeded only by his own incompetence. Later on, it would transpire that the reason he had no experience is that he'd take the client's money and go shopping. I'm not the type to massage egos, so I didn't think he liked me very much. I didn't expect to hear from him again.

The phone rang. It was 2am that night. Do I have a safe house for them to use until their flight out? It took me aback. Why on earth would anyone need a safehouse in fucking Cyprus? I was lying in bed when the phone rang. It was the first time that this had happened, and my missus was pretty shocked. Her 'what the actual fuck' reaction was even stronger than mine. Phone calls at all hours of the day or night were routine to me when I was on mission, and since that time we've both got a bit more used to it happening at home, but at the time I don't think she was too impressed. It was her introduction to the world of child recovery as much as it was mine. I said 'sorry love, I've got to go out', and she was so tired that she gave me a quick 'alright, okay go' and then rolled over, falling straight back to sleep

I headed down to the empty promenade and met up with them by the beach on the main road. They were running an operation in Tunisia, where it turned out that in a stroke of absolute fucking genius Mick had sent two elderly guys, with no experience of either military engagements or covert surveillance, to follow a target and recover a child. If you're following someone and you keep using the same fucking vehicle to do it, they're going to notice after a while. You're going to get followed yourself, possibly by someone who actually knows what they're doing.

Once you're being followed, the worst thing you can do is to have predictable movements. In this case going back to the same hotel and staying in the same place, day after day, probably wasn't the brightest idea. Predictably, they got caught. It turned out that the parent was connected to some kind of Tunisian criminal organisation and took great pleasure in kicking down their hotel doors, torturing them for four or five days and handing them in to the local authorities.

It wasn't until a week or two later before Mick told me the details. After the torture they found themselves locked up in a Tunisian jail and left to rot. I don't know whether they're still there now, or even whether or not they've survived. One of them had a medical condition which couldn't be treated easily over there, and he ran out of meds after a few months. I do know that they were still in that jail a couple of years later. Mick felt responsible, and kept telling me that he was trying to help them. In those intervening years he'd failed with a few recovery operations, leaving himself totally broke, so I'm not quite sure how much help he could be.

Now, Daniel and Mick believed that they could be being tracked by the same people. They were in a state of total panic. Yes, I could fix them up with a safe house. That wouldn't be a problem. But I needed to know that the safe house would indeed be safe.

I told them to put their electronic devices in the bin. It was rather important that they didn't lead anyone straight back to any safe house I could rustle up during the early hours of the morning. Mick had other plans. He'd bought himself an iPhone 5 SE, which at the time was still state-of-the-art technology. He wasn't going to throw that into the bin for the sake of his own personal safety, so instead they rushed straight to the airport and sat in the departure lounge for 14 hours before their flight. Alarm bells were already starting to ring: I could see for myself on the very first day everything that was going to cause me to leave. I mean what the heck? This was another 'joke shop' operation – the equivalent of a 'here's one I made earlier' on the old children's TV programme Blue Peter. I would have to set out to professionalise the whole thing.

A few weeks later, Daniel called me and asked me to fly over to Lebanon for a few weeks as he was hitting dead end after dead end. I got the sense that these dead ends were because they didn't have anyone really with the determination to get it done. Daniel was waiting for his boss to chase things up, and his boss was more interested in going shopping than in chasing anything up, so the whole thing was grinding to a halt. Meanwhile, the child was still being kept in Miriata, a town close to the Syrian border. Still recovering from my injury, and unable to hear out of one ear, I agreed to join the mission.

Chapter 8 -
Gathering intel

"What an amazing magician this Lebanon is" -
Joseph-Ernest Renan

Lebanon is a rich, varied, complex and divided nation. Christian and Muslim; coastal and mountainous; picturesque and polluted, the nation has a richness and charm yet harbouring dark, dangerous people. Its name immediately evokes an image of beautiful cedar trees dominating the landscape, their distinctive needle-leaves providing shade in the most arid of places.

I flew into the ramshackle Beirut airport, being met by Daniel in a big black GMC car. Coming out of the airport, I was greeted by one of the more strange sights I've seen whilst travelling the world: a green layer of mist over the city, caused by air pollution. I felt that pollution, stuck in traffic on the coastal motorway between Beirut and Tripoli. You can feel the thickness of the air pollution, causing you to choke as you breathe in.

It's just a 20-mile drive up the beautiful coastal motorway to our fancy boutique hotel in a Christian town called Byblos, the ancient Phoenician capital. It's one of the oldest surviving cities in the world, dating back maybe seven thousand years, blending ancient and modern. Not that I saw much of that of course: I wasn't there to be a tourist. I was there to rescue a child.

My full briefing on the current situation which I received on arrival at the hotel was unfortunately as I suspected. Nothing had changed, at least in terms of the operational side of the mission. The living situation, though, was slightly different. The mother and the child's grandfather (he was our main point of contact, having hired our company to undertake the rescue) were now allowed, I think by court order, to live with the father in Miriata. The grandfather had freedom of movement, but unfortunately under the Islamic rules governing Miriata, Sarah did not. She had to stay put, and in any case in Hezbollah-controlled territory could not leave without being accompanied by a man. She was basically escorted everywhere she went but she could, I suppose, have left: she was not a prisoner. But if she did so, she would have to leave her child behind – and there would be no guarantee that she could return. The father was also receiving protection on the orders of the town's mullah.

Religion and politics are inextricably linked in Lebanon, with an enforced balance in the Lebanese Parliament between Muslim and Christian politicians. Until 1990, Christians elected 60% of seats and Muslims 40%. After their new Constitution came into force, with a shifting population, it became 50-50. The Muslim community is split between Sunni and Shia, with tensions frequently cropping up between the two. The country itself is not governed by Sharia law, but the "personal status" of Muslims is. Different rules apply to Sunni, Shia, and non-Muslims. A single country, with three different sets of rules governing people in the same territory, is complex: it's perhaps not quite as bad as the arcane Belgian system (with overlapping French, Wallonian and Flemish systems cutting across every level of government, leading to widespread confusion), but it's a close-run thing. Under these circumstances, with the child being located in a Hezbollah-controlled town, legal action was frequently bogged down in red tape. It seemed that direct action was going to be the only way to reverse this kidnapping.

I insisted that we had to drive up to Miriata to get a feel for the ground and do a full recce of the area. I wanted to take some pictures, to get to know the town. I'd need to have a knowledge of where the checkpoints would be, where the police stations would be found, and try to spot the target location without being seen. It wasn't too dissimilar to what we'd done back in Iraq and Afghanistan. If you're going to do any form of security, it pays to know everything about the terrain that you might be fighting on. You need to know which angle trouble could come from, and have everything planned as meticulously as humanly possible.

Daniel had been too afraid to go into the area on his own because it was Hezbollah-controlled, and it certainly wouldn't have been the best of places to meet with the grandfather: there would have been people everywhere. We knew that we couldn't get near the kid, or near Sarah, so he would have to be our point of contact. This would be the first time that Daniel had actually seen the area.

If we got pulled over, it would be rather obvious that we weren't locals. Our appearance, and the fact that we speak only English, would have been dead giveaways. Fortunately, Daniel had a United Nations arm patch which should be enough to get us through. Everything was a case of gathering more information at this stage. This wasn't even the planning phase. It's not possible to plan until you've got the basic information you need to be able to formulate a plan. Whether it's child recovery, client protection, maritime security or a military assault, the fundamentals are essentially the same but with slightly different ingredients. Skills learned in one field can easily be transferred to another.

Having done as much scouting of the area as we could, we drove back down to Tripoli and went to a café called Breakfast to Breakfast. Daniel planned that the grandfather would come to the café to meet us, but there was no way that I could let that happen. After what had happened to their two guys in Tunisia, I certainly wasn't going to take any chances. Presumably they were still languishing in a Tunisian jail, and I'd no intention of experiencing either a Lebanese prison or Hezbollah hit.

I took charge, using my tactical knowledge. Daniel and I were in the café, just the two of us. No, he's not fucking meeting us here. What if he's being followed? No, we have to be more careful than that. Go to a different coffee shop down the road and get a table. Text the grandfather, tell him to order a coffee and sit there by himself. Then send him to come and join you. I'll follow him out at a discreet distance, and make sure that nobody else is tracking him. Everything needs to look natural, doing nothing to arouse any suspicion.

We follow the plan. I identify him coming in. I nurse my drink slowly, waiting to see if anyone else follows him in or pays any attention. He doesn't stop too long, of course. Nobody left the café when the grandfather did. Good. I finish my own drink and casually head out, leaving a few coins on the table as a tip. It's a busy street with all the hustle and bustle of market traders. I browse a few stalls, using my peripheral vision to look out for anything amiss, staying maybe 150 yards away at all times, not allowing a connection to be made between us. There's a boy begging with a pot of chai, approaching passing cars whilst trying to sell pencils or something or other. He's no threat. I continue scanning my surroundings without making it obvious that I'm doing so.

As the grandfather enters the second coffee shop, I wait a moment longer. Once I am absolutely satisfied that it's safe, I go in and sit down with him and Daniel. I sense that the penny has dropped with Daniel. He understands a bit more about just how careful you have to be to keep yourself protected. The irony of it all was that I was using skills I didn't even know that I had. Surveillance and counter-surveillance were more a part of everyday life to me - primarily in Iraq, but also in Afghanistan, where you're constantly on the lookout for anything which could possibly be suspicious. You're always on your guard. If you're doing foot patrols you're observing people, body language, everything that might give you the split-second you need to be able to spot an ambush in time. Operating independently is merely a different application of the same skills.

My mind wandered to the first time the penny really dropped about just how easily military skills could be transferred and then used without thinking. On the parade ground, every soldier is drilled into learning how to do a 'change of arms'. It's a simple, efficient way of switching your weapon from one hand to another. You'll often see a change of arms in front of Buckingham Palace, when a guard on duty will perform one whenever their arm happens to get tired. I always thought that the change of arms was merely ceremonial.

Then, in Baghdad working as a private military contractor, I found myself in the rear-left of a vehicle engaged in action. The clear voice 'Contact Front' came over the radio, and our driver moved us forward past the target. We began shooting almost dead ahead, slightly off to the left. Having gone past the target, we next needed to cover the other two vehicles. After a quick U-turn, the target was now on the right-hand side as we came back towards it.

Instinctively, I performed a change of arms and my weapon was now able to be brought to bear on the same target at the other side. If I'd tried to transfer my gun in a crowded vehicle on the move in any other way, it would have been as awkward as anything. I didn't want to be whacking someone else in the face with my gun during contact with the enemy. It turned out that there was a tactical reason for the skill that I'd learned, if only the Army had bothered to tell me.

I focus back on the situation at hand. I've walked into a basic coffee shop, with chairs scattered around. Hardly a Starbucks: more functional and surprisingly dark, taking my eyes a moment to adjust. There's an olde-worlde sense hanging in the air, the Muslim coffee shop's equivalent of a dark old-fashioned English pub (though nowhere near as nice, in my opinion). I look around, making sure that I know my surroundings. There's a step going up to the next level, and a kitchen area at the back. It's no different to any other coffee shop that you could find in dozens of Islamic countries, which is good because there's no need to appear in any way out of the ordinary.

I could easily get a Turkish coffee, but the menu is no more like a Starbucks than the décor. Don't expect to be able to get a latte. An Americano is just about the only real nod to Western culture, so I order one of those. It's a real battle to get them to understand that I would like some milk to put into the coffee. Not the done thing round here, apparently, and the language barrier doesn't help. I make a mental note to learn the Lebanese word for milk.

Daniel introduces me only as Ryan. There's no need to give my full name; no need to take any chances. It's an unusual situation for both of them, but one which I could easily take in my stride. I size him up: maybe 5 foot 10 or 11, old but with white hair and big teeth. He's of average build, not exactly fat but he has a bit of a belly on him and is clearly unfit. This, I think, will need to be factored into the plan.

First, I listen to the grandfather. He, Oskar, is initially talking about all of his various rescue ideas. I start to wonder why, if he's got so many plans, he doesn't just get on with it and get them done. Soon though, I realise quite how far 'out there' his ideas are. He's not used to this, clearly. He's educated, old, eccentric: the kind of person who gets a cleaner to massage his feet. He'll talk a good talk but hasn't a clue about actual operational security. And he's got a thing about boats, always talking to me about boats. His latest Bond-like plan stems from a time he once hired a 4-metre dinghy with paddles and an electric motor. It was so quiet, he exclaims! Why, he wonders, couldn't we do the same?

I, on the other hand, have some actual experience of those seas from my maritime security work. You want to take a 4-year-old child on a broken 4-metre rhib [Rigid-Hulled Inflatable Boat] out to sea in choppy waters? It would be suicide, to say nothing of the thought of putting a child through that. No. We'll certainly need something substantially better than that.

I become aware that Oskar is going to be something of a challenge. There's something about his personality. He talks a lot, but his words often say very little of much use. At that time, I had no idea of just how much danger Oskar's mouth would eventually put me in. It was time to insist on getting some information. I switched into interrogation mode. I asked questions. Bluntly. It was down to business, taking page after page of notes. If there was anything, however small, that he could tell me, it could be pivotal. I needed to get into details, the main thing that hadn't yet been tried.

Tell me everything about your relationship with your daughter.

Nothing concerning in response to that question. I listen intently, trying to find any hint of dishonesty. I don't sense anything of concern.

Was there any abuse? Was there any domestic violence?

They had their ups and downs, but nothing that would suggest anything like this.

Did we know about any Hezbollah connections before he took the child?

No nothing. He never really talked about it at all.

Why did he decide to leave?

Don't know. He seemed to want to live back in Lebanon.

I feel that there must have been arguments about that, surely, but it's a suspicion that has never been confirmed one way or the other to this day.

Tell me about him?

Gym-fit, well-toned. A beach body type of guy.

Do we know anything about his childhood?

No.

Was he ever abused? Are there any fears of him abusing the child?

Not to Oskar's knowledge.

I ask similar questions to glean information about Sarah and her daughter, then move onto operational matters. The key questions are about the house.

What level of security is there?

There are weapons and guns inside the house, and armed personnel around the house.

What's the layout of the area?

There's an olive grove outside. It's dense enough, but it's an olive grove so there's still space between trees.

Oskar is able to describe the interior of the house, telling me which room is where. That could prove to be gold dust later.

What are the sleeping arrangements?

Oskar shares a room with his daughter, but the child sleeps in the same room as her father.

He would start to drift off, rambling away from the point. Stop. Answer the fucking question. This is what I need to know. The questions must have taken at least an hour, but I was starting to gain some clarity. The first stirrings of a plan were forming in my mind.

Chapter 9 -
Tactical retreat

"Everything will be okay in the end. If it's not okay, it's not the end" - John Lennon

First, we needed to prepare the ground. If there was to be any noise at night, we needed it to seem like it was normal. It would help if we could draw everyone into a false sense of security. If they were woken up in the middle of the night, we didn't want their first thought to be intruders. We wanted their first thought to be "It's that old bloke again, he's just nuts".

He needed to play the part of a senile old man, on the verge of developing dementia. He needed to clash some pans, make some noises, develop the habit of sleepwalking and talking to himself in his sleep. Wake people up at night-time. If it leads to them being a little sleep-deprived, all the better. The more fatigued that they were by the time we were ready to act, the better it would be. I planned, at some point, to try to get eyes on the house itself and to listen to how they reacted to noise. For now though, it wasn't the time to disclose that to Oskar.

The meeting ended cordially enough, and I think that Oskar had some degree of confidence that I would be able to get somewhere even though others had been failing for months. We went our own separate ways, staggering our departure times on the off chance that someone was watching us leave.

Now it was time to get an impression of Miriata at night time. Streets are eerily quiet at night, especially when we were entering new territory. I wasn't there to waste any time, so we headed straight up there again late that night, arriving at around 2am. Hopefully everything would be quiet by then. There's always time to sleep later.

My plan was originally to go up on the Western side of the town, through the mountains and olive groves, skirting around it and then coming at the house from the North. The road, little more than a track, became impassable with debris in our way. We stopped, greeted by the sight of two men with shotguns. Farmers, perhaps, or Hezbollah. Either way, it was clear that we couldn't proceed any further. They wanted to know what we were doing, and by way of explanation Daniel flashed his United Nations badge.

We changed our plan, approaching this time from the East, but again had to turn around as we spotted a military checkpoint in the distance. The only option would be to go directly, which added an element of risk as it meant driving through the town itself – the same route as we'd taken when doing the original recce. As we drove through the town, we noticed some people outside a bakery – the only people we saw at all, next to a rather smart-looking BMW.

We eventually made our way up towards the house, hoping to drive round the back and take a look at the olive grove, but Daniel took a wrong turn – one road too soon - and took us into a dead end. As he did a swift 180, headlights appeared behind us. It was a BMW, probably the same one that we'd already seen whilst driving through the town. The occupants jumped out with shotguns and AK47s, blocking the road just a few metres ahead of us. Now what?

We were unarmed, and we couldn't exactly fight our way out of the situation. We didn't dare to stop, because there wasn't exactly any guarantee that we wouldn't be captured, tortured or even just shot outright if we did. Or they could be robbers. There were so many possibilities. There was really only one option: run. My training, formal and informal, kicked in. I was calm and precise, quickly directing

Daniel to drive towards them, swerving around the car and speeding off as fast as we could in the opposite direction. They probably couldn't start shooting at the car. Too messy.

Speed is always of the essence in these situations. Just like in Iraq, speed is a form of defence. Present a moving target, especially in the dark, and they won't know how to react. They couldn't have known much about who was in our vehicle, and they certainly wouldn't have expected my level of training. They had the element of surprise; we had the military-minded disciplined approach to getting out of the situation quickly and safely.

A few seconds later, we could see headlights again in the rear-view mirror. They didn't know who we were, that was the one positive about the incident. I didn't know, but assumed, that they were protecting the village. They must have seen a strange car, wondered who we were and what we were doing. Maybe they suspected that we were trying to get up to that house. One way or the other, once we'd managed to give them the slip, I knew that we'd have to obtain a different rental vehicle. This one was now compromised.

After we'd headed back to Byblos, and of course changed our vehicle, I spent another week with Daniel. My job was to try to help him figure out his next move. We had a full debrief and another meeting with Oskar. My opinion was simple and straightforward: it was not going to be safe to attempt a rescue from Miriata. One way or another we would need a pretext to get them out of that town – whether on a day trip, a holiday, a shopping visit, or anything else. Fortunately, there were legal proceedings still going on which dovetailed nicely with that advice. The application before the Lebanese courts was to permit a move within Lebanon to a more Westernised part of the country. For an Australian woman to stay with a child in a culture where she was not permitted to leave the house on her own was a total shock to the system.

I went back to Cyprus whilst Daniel was working the case. I'd done everything that I'd set out to do. I had fulfilled my part of the bargain. I'd given him a fresh pair of eyes on the situation, offering him as much expertise as I could in the short time that I was there. I enjoyed a bit of down-time. There were plenty of medical tests and checkups required to keep my insurance up to date. I relaxed into my normal daily life, spending time with my family and taking my son to the beach. I never expected to return to Lebanon, so it was time to relax and recover before taking on whatever my next assignment might be.

Life had always been that way for me: complete the mission, then move on to whatever the universe might throw at me next. One chapter of your life ends, and a new one begins. As far as I was concerned, that was the last of my involvement in child recovery. But life, as it often does, threw a curve ball at me.

Chapter 10 -
Cars and boats and plans

"The difficult is what takes a little time; the impossible is what takes a little longer" - Fridtjof Nansen

That curve ball didn't take long to arrive. Two weeks after I'd left Lebanon, Daniel quit the case. The money was running thin. Being away from friends and family for so long had started to take its toll on him; he'd been there for months without really seeing the progress to justify it.

Daniel had one recent big success though: the Lebanese courts had ruled in their favour when it came to the location of the child. The child would now be moved into a more Westernised area, away from Hezbollah control. Going to court in such a case is like a shot in the dark. Lebanese law is difficult to understand or predict, with elements of the old French legal system and the code Napoleon, going back to the colonial days. It has elements of Ottoman law, and elements of more traditional Middle Eastern Islamic law.

From a tactical point of view, that was a real plus for the mission. The environment we'd be operating in was no longer fully under the kidnapper's control. He wouldn't have the support, weapons and resources of an entire town available to him. The terrain would be more neutral, not of our choosing specifically – but crucially, not of his choosing either. The odds had been evened up, just a little bit. This would now be much closer to a fair fight. I doubt that anyone was under any illusions of the level of difficulty that the mission still presented, however. Nobody had ever successfully recovered a child from Lebanon before. Without being able to secure a passport from the Lebanese authorities, getting the child home would be a monumental task.

The phone rang. Rarely had I been so shocked. It was Mick. I thought he hated me, because I'd refused point-blank to massage his planet-sized ego. Alright, he asked me, can you do me a favour and go over there and finish this case? My first thought: why is he asking me? He explained that Daniel had quit the case. Though he was very careful not to actually say so, it was clear that Mick was in something of a hole and was desperate for my help. I wasn't entirely sure how to react. I didn't fully trust the organisation, but at the same time I did believe in the mission.

Would I be allowed to run the mission properly, without interference? He assured me that I would have full operational charge of the mission. That was a good start. I'd seen enough already to know that I couldn't exactly be totally confident in Mick's recruitment process.

Down to brass tacks. There was one question looming large in the background: do we have the financial resources needed to complete the mission? Not really, but there was enough to give me a fighting chance. I would later learn that they'd been paid around £150,000 for the case. By the time I agreed to take over, it seems that £100,000 or so of the money had been squandered. The only thing they had to show for it was the Lebanese court case result moving the child to a different part of Lebanon. Progress, yes, but hardly a hundred grand's worth of progress. It was clear that my time and budget were going to be limited. It still had a feel of a long shot, but if there's one thing that I love it's a challenge where the odds are against me and nobody would truly expect me to succeed.

If we could manage to get the child into international waters, Mick assured me that he had a contact for the skipper of a boat from the North side of Cyprus. It was a trawler which would be happy to collect the mother and child, helping them to make landfall away from the authorities. I was doubtful, to say the least, that this plan would ever come to anything. For starters, it would create a new problem. You can't just cross the border from the Turkish side of Cyprus to the Greek side.

It felt like he wanted to go round in circles, as though I was listening Oskar's ideas all over again. Mick would always have these ideas. In Stuttgart, he told me that I couldn't possibly get out of Germany by the closest border. Quite the reverse: I needed to be out as quickly as possible, before anyone was even looking for us. If you tell me that something can't be done, I'm the kind of person to go out and do it. I took that one as a challenge. For a later mission in Japan, he told me that I'd have to get out on a boat. You'll never get out by plane, he insisted – yet that's exactly how I did it.

My instinct told me that now wasn't the time to fight this particular battle with Mick. His plan would unravel naturally all on its own, so I paid lip-service to it for a while. There was no actual harm being done, and it would keep him busy and out of the way so that I could get on with the actual business of recovering the child.

After a long discussion, and with some reservations, I finally agreed to take over the mission. I'll admit that I was still a bit raw and naïve when it came to this business. I flew out and checked back in to a different hotel in Byblos. If I had it to do over again, there's no way I'd have been staying in the same area. Too much unnecessary risk. Staying in hotels, too, is often an unnecessary risk. A lot of hotels will take your passport and make a copy of it. That physical record of my presence isn't really safe. Today, I wouldn't dream of staying in any such hotel. I'd sleep in my car, stay with friends in their homes, or stay in a no-frills, no-questions-asked cheap motel.

Now I had complete control over the entire operation. The first order of business was surveillance. I split this into two parts, both of which overlapped a little bit in terms of time and energy. First, I needed to know all the roads and the area like the back of my hand. Second, I had to identify a suitable place on the coastline to manage the extraction. There would be no real chance of taking the child up to Beirut and getting out from there: the distance is too long, and the traffic can be horrific. The best-laid plan could be ruined by something as prosaic as a traffic jam. That idea was out: the situation would not be within my control.

Whilst doing all of this, I met with Oskar. He was able to give me more details on the location of Sarah and her child. They had moved to Jounieh, a town barely a 15-minute drive south of Byblos, and were staying in a hotel. With the child not yet old enough to need to be in school, their movements were fairly functional. Jounieh also had a café in the Breakfast to Breakfast chain. This one was more modern, with a children's play area. The Jounieh branch of Dunkin' Donuts was their other common trip. There was now something of a routine, a pattern which I could work with. I needed to establish and verify that pattern: what time they get up, what time they go to bed, and what times of day they could be at a particular location without arousing any suspicion. Nobody must think that there's anything out of the ordinary until the extraction has already happened. The element of surprise is critical to the success of any military operation, and this carried forward from there.

The biggest positive of the meeting was that Oskar also introduced me to Pieter, a Lebanese Christian who he'd used for translation. Oskar knew nothing about subtlety or subterfuge, telling everyone he met about what his daughter was going through and what they were trying to do. Frankly, it was a massive security risk. It had one upside though: Pieter knew everything about the situation. My first job was to assess whether Pieter was truly on our side: was he a friend and resource, or a huge threat to the whole operation? My first thought was fuck off, I'm not going to trust anyone Oskar's introduced me to.

Pieter was a clean person with short, tidy hair – the kind who frequents the barber's shop recreationally, a cultural part of the laid-back daily life in Lebanon. He always had a couple of days' stubble, as though a conscious choice to keep the stubble as a fashion look. He was always smartly-dressed, very laid back but hugely switched-on, sharp as a button and able to understand the meaning behind my words. There was an instant sense of warmth which came from him. He was a family man with a wife and kids of his own: inherently trustworthy, having a deep sense of empathy with Sarah for the horrible situation she found herself in. He was someone I could work with. I could sense that much instantly, but trust? Trust is something which needs to be earned. I'm not going to risk my life based upon an instinctive sense.

I had to make that assessment as quickly as I could. It would be much easier to use someone who knew the story and was onside. Over the next week, he was able to prove himself in little ways. I needed a local phone that was untraceable, not connected to my name or anyone else's. If I tried to buy one as an outsider, I'd have to hand my passport over – which really would ruin the whole point of having a burner phone. Pieter sorted it instantly. I gradually started to feel as though I had a professional operator with me 24/7, someone who was motivated by the case. You could see that within him.

At the same time, we started looking for boats. We went down to a few marinas, looking for a solid, reliable 4 to 6 metre rhib. It needed to be good enough to get across those waters, but we kept getting offered clapped-out 25-year-old dinghies on the cusp of falling to pieces. It was no, no, no. But Pieter kept trying and was able to be discreet about it. I liked that. More traditional approaches, like walking into a boat shop and just buying a boat, ran into a couple of problems. The price tag was probably over budget, but what really put paid to that plan was the registration. Whatever we did had to be untraceable.

I had to bear in mind that Pieter had never done anything like this before. Whilst I had the experience of Iraq and Afghanistan, for all his undoubted intelligence Pieter didn't have that soldier's instinct. He wasn't ex-military, so his first thought was straightforward: let's go ask in the marina to get a boat.

If there's one thing you learn after years in maritime, it's that where there's a harbour or a marina, there's mafia. I was about to be introduced to the Lebanese equivalent: the shady underground no-questions-asked kind of people who could make anything or anyone disappear for a price. I told them I need a boat because I'm trying to remove a package from the country, no questions asked. How much is it going to cost me? They told Pieter to wait outside. Every piece of electronic equipment was taken away from me. They stripped me down to my boxers, presumably checking that I wasn't wearing any recording equipment. I suppose they were only doing what I always do: making absolutely certain that they were safe. Street-smart and savvy, but a little unnerving all the same. They could have just dragged me out of that building and I would have disappeared without a trace. This cocky Westerner who confidently strode into their office, telling them I needed a job doing, would never have been heard of again.

What's in it for them to do that? Nothing. They quote me £25,000. It's an option at least. I call Mick and ask him whether we can get that kind of money together. No, sorry.

I tried a small fishermen's harbour in a traditional village just south of Tripoli, making friends with an ex-body builder turned tuna fisherman. I built up a rapport with him over a couple of weeks, even going out on his boat and catching fish with him. What, I asked when I judged that I knew him well enough to drop the bombshell, would it take for you to help me get into international waters and meet another boat? Unfortunately it was an absolute no-go. He was a devout Muslim, feeling that to do so would be a breach of his faith. Besides, he couldn't risk losing his fishing licence. I had to burn my bridges and cut off contact, not able to risk going back.

One avenue after another was proving unfruitful. The frustration continued to grow. I spoke over the phone to the Turkish captain, more for Mick's benefit than anything else, trying to persuade him that he needed to be prepared to go into a port. He refused point-blank, being fearful of doing so. That plan was dead in the water: there was now nothing happening on either side of the water.

Whilst all this was ongoing, I kept up my surveillance of Sarah and her child. I became a regular customer of both Breakfast to Breakfast and Dunkin' Donuts, sitting quietly and unobtrusively in a corner nursing a hot dog and a coffee or something similar. I'd often be close enough to hear what Sarah was saying to her daughter. I'd keep eyes on the hotel whenever I could, often sitting in a dirt-track car park just around the corner to watch their movements and glean any more information that I possibly could. I'd sit there for five minutes after they'd gone in, then slowly drive off. One day I pulled out, and headlights appeared behind me almost immediately. My spider senses started to twitch, feeling that I was being followed.

Fuck. How do I get rid of this vehicle? How do I know what it is? Is it a government vehicle? Is it Hezbollah? Are they connected to the father in some way? There were many questions, but it was most important to deal with the imminent threat. I'd normally turn towards Route 51 and head out onto the dual carriageway that passes for a highway, just one major junction away from my hotel in Byblos. This time, though, I wanted to check if I was being followed. I took an earlier turning than usual. For the first time, my acquired knowledge of the local roads came in handy. I led them on a winding mountain road. As it bent right then left, I'd be out of their view for a few seconds. The moment that happened, my foot was straight down to the floorboards and I shot forward. There's a point which could be used as a turning circle not much further on, so I turned my vehicle right around. As I drove back, there were two guys sitting in the car. Our eyes connected as they drove past, staring straight into each other's faces – at least, as much as could be seen in the dusk of the evening.

I was pretty sure that they were following me, but now to make sure. What if it's just a normal car that happened to be heading in that direction? A thought came into my head: Jason Bourne. He'd park the car up, turning all the lights off, and wait. If they drive back past, I'll know that they're following me - why else would someone be doing a U-turn on a mountain road after following me for a few minutes already? I turned to park next to a row of cars outside an apartment block, switched off the lights. The Bourne connection in my mind reminded me to take my foot off the brake. Nobody must see brake lights as they drive past.

I had a hesitant feeling, the start of paranoia. By the time the Lebanon mission was done, it took me months to get back to normal because I was that emotionally fucked up from it. I'd have the constant feeling of being watched, that someone was going to come and take revenge after I'd successfully recovered Sarah and her daughter. It's when you pause, just for a moment, that all those feelings come to the fore. The adrenaline keeps you going until then.

I was jolted out of my thoughts as the same car drove straight past. I reversed back out of the parking area, and came right back up their arse. I was in a Chevy Suburban, so I'm looking down on their smaller car. I drive up behind them, flashing my lights and sounding my horn. It's the fear factor. Now it's my turn to put the shits up them. I want them to know they've been spotted and that I'm following them. My morale's been pretty low after every setback recently. I can't let this fucking shit happen. They need to know they've got a fight on their hands if they come after me.

Shit. They've turned the corner, headed towards Route 51. There are only two ways they can go from here: one heads across a bridge, and the other takes you to Byblos. I don't want them to go to Byblos. I don't want them to connect me to Byblos in any way, shape or form. I'm right up on his bumper. I learned how to drive on Route Irish by ramming cars off the road at 120mph. Now my training kicks in. I smash into the back of him, push him beyond the junction. When a car this size rams you, you're going forward no matter what. I veer off onto Route 51 myself to head towards Byblos.

I'm able to relax. I've been hitting so many brick walls, so many promising leads that turn out to be what the Americans would call a nothingburger. Is child recovery really so specialised that I can't do this? How am I going to get a child out in these circumstances? My thoughts are 'mate, there ain't no way'. Maybe I should walk, but Daniel has already walked. If I leave, who's going to save this child?

Chapter 11 -
Do you know who I am?

"And when they spy on us, let them discover us loving" - Alice Walker (Taking the arrow out of the heart)

Life is complex. Anyone will tell you that. Even as I'm writing the story of what happened, I'm constantly questioning why something happened. In such a bizarre situation, bizarre things happened: the child went to Miriata for a couple of weeks to stay with the father. This seemed to all have been pre-arranged and everything was in order. Sarah would head back to Norway for a while over Christmas, then the child would be returned to the hotel and everything would resume.

By the time this happened, I'd been back in Lebanon for a fortnight or so. It gave me the opportunity, finally, to meet Sarah. We had to be exceptionally careful, as ever, to be sure that she wasn't being followed. When we met, we met in a touristy spot in Byblos. The town has a rich cultural heritage. It's the real deal, it's got a castle and everything. We met in one of those Souk-type marketplaces which just exudes character, and where the more naïve tourists will be ripped off whilst locals haggle mercilessly – if they shop there at all.

The first thing I notice is her accent, as you'd expect from a Norwegian who had a child in Australia and now lives unexpectedly in Lebanon. I notice the Aussie twang within a Scandinavian accent, though I can barely detect any Lebanese influence in there yet. It's an odd mix. She's got lightish-brown hair, is in her early-to-mid twenties, and she's fit. You can tell that she usually goes to the gym, so it's a bit ironic really that she seems to spend half her life in Dunkin' Donuts at the moment. But what hits me, more than anything, is that actually nothing really hits me about her. Sarah's just an average person who's been caught up in an impossibly difficult situation. You can sense the sadness in her eyes, though she's trying to hide it. There's makeup trying and failing to cover her obvious tiredness, and you wonder just how much of a toll this is taking on her mental health. Like looking at an iceberg, I could only "see" the surface that she was willing to show me. She smiled, but the smile seemed to be forced – not fake, but the smile of someone who has to make a conscious effort not to allow the sadness to creep through during every waking hour.

Her words, mannerisms and body language show that she's absolutely devoted to her father. It's not that he was controlling or anything, but more that she looked up to him. Perhaps it's because he was the only one who'd been trying to help. Perhaps she simply believes in his far-fetched plans, or maybe she just wants something to be able to cling onto, some thought of comfort. I don't know. This could be anyone.

She's no introvert, but my abiding memory of Sarah is just that she's a normal person. She could be anyone. This is something which could happen to anyone, anywhere, at any time in the event of a breakup with a partner who decides to put their will above the child's. If you know it's going to happen, you might get an order to prevent travel, but more likely than not the child's out of the country before you have a clue that anything's amiss.

"Do you recognise me? Have you ever seen me before?"

That was my first question to her. I'd spent so much time in Breakfast to Breakfast and Dunkin' Donuts whilst she was there, that I was slightly surprised when she said no. I'd been so close to them that I could hear her talking to her daughter and what they were discussing. It was a great confidence boost right there, showing me that my surveillance had been as subtle as it was effective. I'd be sitting there watching football, eating a hot dog and drinking a coffee whilst she was playing with her kid in the toy area.

When doing such surveillance, it's important to blend into the background whilst doing everything that you can to change your appearance to limit the chance of being noticed. That might be something as simple as wearing a baseball cap, wearing a different style of clothes, switching between shaven and unshaven, or any of a number of subtle things you can do to look different without attracting any attention.

Sarah was shocked to learn that I'd seen her so many times, and possibly slightly disturbed by the thought, but the more she thought about it the more she was comforted to know that someone on her 'side' had been there, watching over her, even though she didn't know. If you believe in any form of spiritual world, in God or angels, maybe there's a metaphor somewhere for us being watched over also without even realising it. It would transpire later that the child's father didn't know anything about me at all. It showed that my professionalism had paid off.

She also told me about another child recovery company, one of Mick's competitors, which she'd spoken to over the phone. There was an email chain between them and Sarah, and Mick was able to confirm that there had been contact with another company but as far as he was concerned it was over now. The last thing I wanted was to be tripping over someone else's work. At the time, I thought no more about it – but this detail would later turn out to be far more critical than we'd realised.

The conversation continued with more of the same questions that I'd asked Oskar. I asked how she was feeling, and she shrugged her shoulders. She said simply that it is what it is, whether she likes it or not. I probed further, checking that there was nothing abusive –

nothing that set off any alarm bells to suggest that she could be in any imminent danger. That was a relief, because it meant that the operation could take as long as it needed to. It was affecting her mental health, that much was clear, so I was keen to avoid any undue delay.

She wasn't able to offer any more details or information which could be of any practical operational use. At least, though, we'd now met and she wouldn't panic too much when it came time to extract her daughter from the country. Whilst the father had temporary custody, Sarah was going back to Norway for a fortnight to spend Christmas with her family. It was clear that she needed a break, some R&R, before heading back into this situation. It would have been soul-destroying to sit around in a hotel simply waiting for the return of her daughter. The meeting had been an important one, but it didn't fundamentally change anything.

Later that night, I went for a few drinks in a bar in Byblos to clear my head. It's something I do from time to time: my best ideas tend to come either when I'm having a few drinks or just as I'm drifting off to sleep. Somehow, once I'm able to rid my mind from all the clutter which it acquires through the day, my subconscious is able to process things. That's where the 'lightbulb above the head' moments come from. Don't think I'm advising you that the solution to every problem is sleep and alcohol though. I'm not. Alcohol is only a solution in chemistry.

Surprisingly, Sarah ended up in the same bar as me. She was normally more of a party person, but today she'd gone somewhere quiet because - unsurprisingly - she wasn't really in that kind of mood. If anything, she'd probably gone for a few drinks so that she wasn't all alone in a country she neither knew nor had ever planned to visit. Neither of us were being followed, I'd established that, so screw it. I went over and talked to her. I did everything I could to comfort her. I'm here to sort this out, I told her. I was as reassuring as it was possible for anyone to be when they didn't have a plan.

Over the previous few weeks, I had developed a sense of urgency about the mission. The Sassine Square in Beirut is the beating heart of the city, a melting-pot of cultures, where Sunni and Shia Muslims and Christians often mix, tourists are likely to visit, and the cash registers rarely stop ringing. On October 19th, 2012, in an alleyway not far from the square in a Greek Orthodox Christian area, a massive car bomb exploded. The blast left a huge crater in the road, killing at least four people and injuring over a hundred more as the debris scattered over an area of more than quarter of a mile. Paul Salem's article for the Carnegie Middle East Centre reported that a Lebanese Major-General had been killed, and that the force of the blow was the equivalent of 50 kilograms of TNT.

The attack had a significant effect on the people of Byblos, becoming the talk of the town for months afterwards. As Byblos was a Christian town with significant tourism, the locals felt a sense of affinity with the Greek Orthodox community in that area of Beirut. It shook people up: partly because of the tragedy of a situation unfolding just an hour's drive from them, but also because of a feeling that terrorism was now closer to home. If it could happen in a tourist part of Beirut, why not Byblos? There was a heightened level of anxiety in the area, and it's fair to say that my concerns about Sarah and her daughter's safety were growing, though without any actual concrete threat.

Before Sarah went back to Norway, I met Oskar one more time. He was trying to tell me about the electric boat, over and over again. He was so adamant that he dragged me down to the harbours, looking at boats that I'd already seen. I was getting more and more frustrated. The more frustrated I got, the more sweary my mind became. It was a fucking waste of my time. I'm done with this guy.

He called me down onto the beach. We were standing together, looking out to sea. As though it was going to prove his point, he pointed across the water and said "Look out to sea. It's just over there." It was 100 or so nautical miles, not at all visible, so I'm not sure that it was exactly going to prove his point. This is suicide, I thought – not for the first time. I started running through the plan in my head. It was, to use a technical military term, shit. No. It was fucking shit. Mick thought we had a Turkish boat in place, but we didn't. The captain was terrified. We couldn't find a properly seaworthy boat in Lebanon. I'm just so fucking done with all this shi…

And that's when I had my epiphany. The answer was so simple. It had been staring me in the face all along. I know loads of places on the Greek side of Cyprus which sell boats. There's a simple reason why that basic point had escaped me. In the contracting business, they'd give me the outline of a plan, and then it was up to me to make that plan work in whatever way I chose. They'd tell me what to do, and I'd put it into practise. Here, I was trying to do the same thing. Instead, I needed to throw everything away. Management in the contracting industry generally have at least some vague clue of what they're doing. But here, Mick didn't. I needed to totally erase that plan from my head and start completely from scratch.

If I found a boat in Greek Cyprus, I know plenty of ex-squaddies who'd be only too happy to help. I'd be able to use my people. They're people I can trust, people who've been in the same bloody battles as me and we've always had each others' backs. That's when you really know you can trust someone, when your lives are both on the line and you're still there working together. It was just the basic concept but it gave me the impetus I needed to finally make some progress. It was time for me to hop back on a flight to Cyprus and find myself a boat captain. And, as an added bonus, I'd be home to see my wife over Christmas. Not much point in staying in Lebanon when nobody else connected to the case would actually be there, anyway.

I'd told Mick that I would be calling the shots if I agreed to take on this mission, so I needed to do so. This was my operation, so I needed to remember that and do it my fucking way from now on.

Now there was a spring in my step. I was flying home on a mission. It was also a strange feeling, because it was the first time I'd had a mission in a truly civilian environment – and even more so when it was in my back yard. Work in Somalia? Coup. Iraq, Afghanistan? War. Maritime? Piracy. And despite the veneer of Christmas decorations in the tourist destinations in Byblos, even Lebanon had Hezbollah and military checkpoints all over the place. For the first time in my career, I didn't need to lurk in the shadows. I could openly approach people. I knew the area, knew the people, and the type of reactions I'd get. Finally, I had something to look forward to.

Chapter 12 -
Loose lips

"Common sense is not so common" - *Voltaire*

My plane hit the tarmac back in Cyprus. I was home, which would normally mean a break from everything. I had been looking forward to seeing my family, and it felt good to be back. I got my first taste of working using home as a base. Looking back, I suppose getting used to spending more time at home was great practice for the mind-numbing tedium of lockdowns. I love spending time with family, but I also go stir-crazy stuck in the same situation. I need something different, something challenging, a change of scenery and ideally some action to get the adrenaline pumping.

The next day, I was straight onto the task of finding a boat and captain. I made a beeline for Larnaca marina to see which captains were around. I walked around, taking care about who to approach – and, more importantly, who not to approach. Loose lips sink ships. Never was that more literal to me than on this mission. It was a needle in a haystack job, so patience was indicated. I found nobody on the first day.

I was about to go and cast my metaphorical nets another time, when a big local businessman – a contact of the family – agreed to meet. He was able to put me in touch with a captain. Based upon the recommendation, I got a meeting immediately. It was a cagey affair, because neither of us trusted each other. I tried to avoid getting into details of the mission, and didn't even mention that the destination was Lebanon, but I did tell him of the need to equip the boat with radar. It spooked him somewhat, but after I explained that I'm ex-military and the mission involved rescuing a kidnapped child, his demeanour softened a little. The nature of this business is a big trigger point for a lot of people's hearts.

He still wasn't going to help me, but suddenly he knew a guy who could. He arranged a meeting with his contact at a local coffee shop. Meetings in Cypriot coffee shops usually involve mafia in one way or another, not that I knew it at the time. Having been passed around from pillar to post, a chain of contacts, finally I was one step away from a real dodgy geezer. The meeting was a huge success because his connection to the leading mafia boss on the island meant he could get pretty much anything he wanted done.

This encounter was different: I knew right away that I was going to get some support from him. More to the point, his lips were sealed. Back in 1986, Sicilian mafiosi Salvatore Ercolano was facing trial in Palermo. Taking the tight-lipped reputation of the original mafia to the extreme, he literally sewed his own lips shut to symbolise the fact that he wasn't going to say anything.

The whole plan started to move quickly – so quickly that I could barely believe how things had changed in such a short space of time. Within a fortnight, Mick had flown into Cyprus. Oskar was on his way across. We'd bought a boat, a 6.4 metre rhib, in great condition – with no incriminating paperwork. A couple of new engines allowed us to double the boat's straight-line speed in case of anyone trying to intercept us before we reached international waters. We had a frame built into the hull to raise up the radar, and a fish finder so that we could plausibly look like we might be a fishing vessel.

Now the problem became one of logistics. My experience in the British Army stood me in good stead for that: the Army does logistics better than almost anyone else in the world. They're quick, efficient and most importantly cheap. It's no surprise that when it came to the rollout of Covid vaccines, the North East (which hired a top retired Army officer to do the job) got it spot on from the start and raced ahead of other regions.

For me, the sequencing was going to be complicated. The mafia would deal only with me. We needed to use two boats, this small one to get us out of Lebanon, and a larger one to slip us through customs without attracting any suspicion. That's where the mafia's yacht came in handy. They knew exactly how to get into a marina whilst customs pretended not to notice. The weather conditions needed to be right for a crossing, so the timing of the extraction depended upon the weather. The rhib would need to be ready and waiting in Lebanon, and I'd need to be there ready to make a move at short notice.

The whole operation now became a bit like one of those logic puzzles where everything has to be sequenced in the correct order. It's a higher-level version of the problem where you've got to get the fox, chicken and grain across the river all at the same time. Each element had to be in place at once. Every part of the plan had to come together, but each part was dependent upon another one.

I now needed to assemble my team. I had just one other guy in mind. My fucking guy. He was the perfect man for the job, an old military contracting buddy: an ex-coxswain and ex-marine. He could drive a boat and knew how to handle himself. That's pretty much all I needed. The smaller the team, the more nimble and agile it is.

Chris was mad, crazy and funny as fuck. Back in the 1980s, television bosses weren't sure about the Mad Murdock character from the A Team. They thought he would be too 'out there', too crazy, too nuts to be a believable and relatable character. He was just too over-the-top, too much of a caricature. It took a serious amount of arm-twisting and persuasion to get the character to go on screen. Nope, not at all. Truth is often much stranger than fiction – and Mad Murdock was more like a toned-down version of Chris. If only you could just tone his character down a bit. He'd drink and drink and drink. As a drinker he was a lover not a fighter, and fucking hilarious to boot. He'd just got divorced, so I could tell that there was a part of him which was a little down – but military banter is military banter, infectious and drawing you in.

Mick got involved, developing the selective amnesia which seemed to plague him so often. He managed to forget that he'd said this was my mission operationally, and decided to throw a spanner in the works by assigning 'House' to the mission. As if almost fucking Stuttgart up wasn't enough, Mick wanted House to almost fuck Lebanon up too. Great. (The Stuttgart and Lebanon timelines overlapped in reality, but if I'd told the story as it actually happened I doubt most readers would have stood the slightest chance of understanding much of what on earth was actually going on.)

I met up with Mick quite a few times over those critical days, but I was updating him rather than involving him with the planning. He couldn't organise the proverbial drinking contest in a brewery. Oskar, the grandfather, also headed over to Cyprus and wanted to be involved with everything. Mick and I set up a meeting with him in a Starbucks. It was in a tourist area, but no more than a stone's throw away from the marina where every dodgy character would congregate.

We arrived to find Oskar sitting in the café with two young girls, spilling his guts and telling them the whole story and how we were planning to rescue his daughter. As we queued up for our coffees we could hear pretty much every word that he was saying – and saying it in a loud, booming voice that anyone in the fucking Starbucks could hear. I stared at him angrily as much as I could to give him a not-so-subtle hint that he needed to shut the fuck right up. If looks could kill, he'd have dropped dead on the spot. What kind of person would start shooting his mouth off just yards away from the place where all the shit was going to happen?

This was in Cyprus. Cyprus is a relatively small nation, with a population about the same as that of Birmingham. In Larnaca, everyone knows someone who knows someone who knows someone. It's a different culture, operating by word of mouth as much as anything. This 'shooting from the lip' could easily have compromised the entire mission. Worse than that, he was shitting right on my doorstep. I had my own family there, and our own safety to think about.

"What – the – fuck – are – you – doing?" That's what I asked him the moment that I could extricate him from the situation. Here he was, talking about a secret operation in public. "You're gonna fucking get me killed on my own doorstep, you prick", I explained to him, about as politely as it sounds. Back in the Army and military contracting days, I'd learned something called OpSEC – Operational Security. We use the same principle of OpSEC all the time in child recovery. It's all about ensuring that nothing you do could potentially fall into the hands of anyone who could want to do you harm, or give away any information which could impact on the success of your mission.

I had to explain the concept of OpSEC to Oskar in a nutshell: "Keep your mouth shut and don't fucking tell anybody anything." Don't blurt it out to random strangers you happen to meet in a fucking Starbucks. And yeah, I'm getting sweary, but I think I'm entitled. Incredibly,

Oskar wanted to meet the mafia guy in charge of the yacht. I mean, don't get me wrong, I do understand that he wanted to be reassured that everything was under control. But does he think that they're the kind of people who would want to be openly introduced to as many people as possible? They wouldn't speak to Mick. They wouldn't speak to Oskar.

They certainly wouldn't be interested in talking to someone whose idea of being tight-lipped was spilling the beans to some random girls in a Starbucks. They wanted a single point of contact, and that contact was me. For them as well as for me, it was far less risky that way.

With hindsight, I think maybe I can understand Oskar's attitude a little better. He was desperate to have some feeling of being in control, to be able to pretend that he had some kind of power over a situation where he was personally no more than a bystander. Oskar probably wanted a sense of pride, to be able to feel that this operation wouldn't be going ahead if it weren't for him. And truthfully it wouldn't, but that's more about the fact that he hired us and bankrolled the project. He hadn't learned that it's a bit like a circus: you can book the acts, but don't expect to be able to tell them which way they should jump during their routine.

By now, we were on the final leg of the planning phase. We'd run tests on the water to check the boat out. We needed to know how much fuel it was going to need to get from Cyprus to Lebanon for starters, how long the crossing was likely to be, and whether the boat was likely to make it there in one piece.

As much as I didn't particularly care for House, I really didn't want to lose Chris – or my escape plan – if anything happened to the boat.

Chris had found his patience wearing thin at various points, and always referred to House as a "useless cunt" when talking about him afterwards.

The boat was looking pretty sharp. The rhib needed to undertake a long crossing, and would have quite a lengthy mission, so I didn't head back out to Lebanon until the boat had already been launched. The last night before the boat departed, we headed out for a good old military tradition: a few drinks at the bar before shipping out. There was an excitement, a tension – the feeling that this shit was about to go down. It's a feeling that I'd known many times before, in a different context.

What really hit home, though, was being up at 4am the next morning to see the boat launched. My missus comes with me to see them off before dropping me off at the airport, and Chris and House get on the boat. It looked absolutely fantastic and everything, but I'm still nervous. It's still a small boat. They would have to fight the weather continuously, and refueling out at sea was going to be interesting to say the least. The crossing was between 12 and 14 hours, an agonising length of time to be waiting to hear from them and to find out that they'd made it safely.

There were certainly some nerves. I didn't stop around to worry about that though. I was straight on the next plane back to Beirut, getting ready to put the last little bits of the plan into motion. I chose the same little boutique hotel in Byblos for Sarah that I'd previously stayed at with Daniel. There were a few reasons for that choice of hotel. In the military, it's usually a sensible idea to choose terrain you know. I knew the layout of the hotel and how it works. The escape plan would require a little more thought and detail, because we hadn't been even considering that hotel for an extraction at the time we were there.

Sarah and her daughter had been in Miriata at that time. There were little details to iron out later once I arrived: the fire exit and checking we could get a vehicle around the back for starters.

Oskar's loose lips played into my hands on this one too. Because it was such a small hotel, there were only a few staff. Oskar had told the two receptionists all about the mission when he stayed there before, but at least it was a long time before any of the details were known. That was probably a good sign because it meant that the staff wouldn't be totally surprised at anything going off. They'd seemed sympathetic, so certainly we weren't expecting any actual hostility towards us.

As I was in the air on my way from Larnaca to Beirut airport, the rhib was making its way across some choppy seas from Larnaca to the port of Beirut. The cover story was so laughably shit that it would undoubtedly be believed.

If the port authorities asked them what the fuck they were doing in a small rhib in Lebanon, their plan was to say that they'd come across on a drunken bet to see whether they could make it across and spend a week fishing. It was just so outrageous, so ridiculous, that nobody was likely to think of it as being a cover story. They'd believe it precisely because it sounded so bizarre.

I knew what they'd be doing. Round about now, the boat would need refuelling. They couldn't exactly hop round to the nearest petrol station and fill up, in the middle of a hundred nautical miles of open sea. Instead, they'd have to refuel the boat themselves whilst on the move. That meant opening up the engines and pouring fuel into the outboard motors from jerry cans whilst the boat was being tossed about by the waves. Not my problem. Chris was perfectly capable of handling that little detail, and the guys at the marina had made sure they had plenty to spare on the boat. By the time they reached Beirut harbour, they'd be able to get hold of more fuel. Finally, it felt like we were getting somewhere.

Chapter 13 - Under the boardwalk

"All warfare is based upon deception" -

Ancient Chinese philosopher Sun Tzu

Another day, and another flight into Beirut airport. I was starting to know the place all too well, and in a small airport it turned out that they also knew me. As I came through customs, I handed over my passport to be scanned. He must have seen that I'd been there before, and asked me whether I have a second passport. That was a question I could answer honestly: no. Are you sure? Yes, I'm sure. Having more than one passport can come in handy, but back then the thought of getting a second one had never really occurred to me.

Something felt wrong though, and the paranoia stepped up a little more. More alarm bells started to ring. I didn't know why there were these additional questions, but nothing could be allowed to leak out. If I was being followed by Lebanese police, there's no way that I could reasonably know about it. Sarah hadn't spotted me following her, which was good, but if someone were following me like that I think I'd know about it. If the police are following you though, they've got the resources to have a full-blown team on the case. They'll have a different person following you every day, or every hour if necessary. You've got no chance of putting it all together and pinging them.

I met up with Pieter at the hotel. My first job was to scan the hotel, checking out the fundamentals of an escape plan. We needed to know that the fire exits actually worked, where exactly they led to, and hopefully that they weren't alarmed. Would it be possible for us to post someone in the breakfast area, open to the public, without arousing suspicion? A lot of questions were answered by careful questions posed to the receptionists. "What do I do if there's a fire?" just comes across as though I'm the kind of person who's obsessed with health and safety. It doesn't necessarily scream out at the person hearing the question that I'm planning to un-kidnap a child by rushing them through the fire exit. Even if it did, the hotel staff who knew had seemed quite sympathetic towards Oskar and Sarah's plight. As regards the fire exits fortunately, yes, everything was perfectly in order.

The hotel was ideal in one sense because Oskar had already been talking to them, so when we did look like we were planning stuff it didn't look out of the ordinary to them. I mean, they already knew we were planning stuff, right? If they hadn't shopped us to any authorities before, they weren't about to start now. And they wouldn't really know, at least at this stage, that it was going to go down right there in their hotel. Words came out of Oskar's mouth like diarrhoea usually comes out of a cow's arse, and usually the diarrhoea was less messy. On this occasion, at least I could turn it to our advantage for once. We were able to ascertain that there wouldn't be any CCTV footage of our route out. The plan was simple enough: to pick up Sarah and the child from the toilets on the day they arrived, take them through the breakfast area, down the fire escape and to a vehicle waiting outside. Their luggage needed to contain nothing of any interest or value because it was going to be jettisoned on arrival.

I couldn't tell Oskar about what had happened at the airport, because it would be even worse if that little fact had leaked. Unfortunately for him, the lack of security meant that I had to keep him pretty much in the dark about what was actually happening until it happened.

The boat was due to arrive in Beirut at any time now. I tried everything to get hold of them, knowing that after a 12-14 hour crossing it was likely that they should be arriving. There was an agonising silence. I waited and waited, and it wasn't until around 10pm – 18 hours after they'd left Cyprus – that they finally got some signal. They'd arrived, but had been stuck in 'traffic' waiting to be given the okay to approach Beirut harbour. That was a relief. The crossing had been a reasonably worrying one. At least now we knew that the journey was possible, so going the other way would be practical. Chris had his orders, so after a brief contact to check that everything was okay, I didn't need to get in touch again until I had the co-ordinates for the point on the coastline where they would need to pick us up.

Chris was going out to sea every day. He was looking for coastguards, military vessels, anything and everything that could possibly hinder us. There were United Nations vessels somewhere at sea, and Americans would be expected off the coast of Israel but they often stray across into Lebanese waters. There might even be Russians out there. Day by day they went out, scouting around, getting used to the weather and tides and seeing what they could get away with.

More importantly, they wanted to piss the Beirut radar operator off. They needed to be seen in the area on a regular basis so that it wouldn't be out of the ordinary when they were somewhere around the coast on the day of the extraction. If all of a sudden there's a random boat, it'll alert the authorities. If it's just two fucking idiots knocking around who've been there for a week or two making total fools of themselves, they'll know who it is. Nobody's going to suspect that those clowns who shouldn't be anywhere near a boat are in fact the lynchpins of a sophisticated clandestine international recovery operation.

In the meantime, they had a few repairs to do. The metal frame we'd used to install the radar was cutting into the fiberglass, wearing it away. Once they got themselves back underway, they learned some valuable information. If they got a tuna fishing licence for that day, nobody would give a damn about them heading out to sea. They'd get told off when they went inland, so they went inland whenever they had a suitable opportunity in order to keep the radar operator in a constant state of utter pissed-offness. That worked well enough as a plan, but it had one rather big downside. The boat got slapped with a 15:00 curfew every single day. Now our time was limited: if we were to go past the 15:00 mark by any significant margin, it would be Game Over for any kind of operation that day. That being said, leaving after 15:00 would mean a night crossing anyway. We wanted this to go down in the morning, so hopefully it wouldn't really matter too much.

Whilst they were busy on the boats, Pieter and I were busy scanning the coastline. Another stroke of luck: the perfect place presented itself, just a 5-minute drive from the hotel. Someone must have once had a boat moored there, because there were a number of steps going down from a small clifftop straight into the water. There was a horseshoe of rocks surrounding the area, breaking the waves naturally. It looked to us as though it was going to be an ideal place to embark because the waters would be calm, and nobody would be able to see. The cliff would keep us hidden from the authorities, and better still it didn't really look like the boat was coming around land. I wrote down the coordinates. I now needed to know from Chris whether the location was suitable from his perspective: could he get the boat in there or not? Could he hold it steady whilst we got everyone on board?

We had three burner phones each. They were never to be used, but left on at all times until they were needed. After my experience at the airport there was no fucking way I was going to take the risk of telling him the location over the phone or send him a text message. Yes, it was probably safe, but I didn't want to create any communication trail that I didn't have to. Just because something is "probably" safe doesn't mean that it's "definitely" safe. You're probably not going to get your brains blown out if you play Russian roulette either, but you'd have to be fifty fucking shades of moronic to actually do it because you reckon a five-in-six chance of survival is okay.

I arranged the meeting by text message for a KFC a reasonable drive away from Byblos, possibly the least likely location for a covert operation – and therefore, a highly appealing one. Also, there would be fried chicken. That was a plus point too. I walked in, ordered food, and casually left the piece of paper with the coordinates on the tray. Chris shook his head at me for not clearing up my mess as I left, walked over and put the tray in the bin. He conveniently picked up the piece of paper as he did so. Can we meet at this place?

Yes, came the reply some time later. I took out the sim card, cut it up and dropped phone and sim card in separate bins. In the meantime I'd scanned some other places, finding alternative coordinates just in case he said no. I needed secondary and tertiary locations in any case in the event of any fuck-up on the day.

The huge bad news though was that the child's father had apparently received a tip-off that someone could be planning to rescue his daughter. I already knew from Sarah that Oskar had approached a number of different child recovery companies. Now it turned out that one particular company had reached out to the father and discussed the case.

Whenever there's a new child recovery case, it's standard operating practice to send out a questionnaire. They want to know details about you, who the kid is, who the kidnapper is, and so on. You need some basic information up front in order to have an idea of how to quote for the operation. It gives you a basic guide to the plan and any legal issues that might arise. In my case, I also reserve the right to turn the operation down altogether. If it's not absolutely clear-cut that the client is in the right, I'm not going to risk my life and limb because in that situation a successful recovery might make an already bad situation worse.

Some of the child recovery companies are fucking cowboys though. They don't give a stuff about anything but money. Pounds, dollars or euros, they'll take them all. If they don't get their cash, they're going to get pissed off. They're little more than thugs for hire, pretending to be there for child recovery and giving our industry a bad, shady name. This particular prick wanted the business, but Oskar had chosen to go with Mick instead. Motivated by pure spite or maybe greed, because I can't think of any other fucking reason he'd do it, Mick's competitor contacted the child's father and tipped him off about the operation. Maybe he charged for information about standard operating practices and how to counter our plans. I don't know. But the father had been tipped off that there's going to be a company out there doing this and doing that. The day before the operation was due to go down, the father came to the hotel where Sarah was going to be staying and did his own recce.

Me and Pieter were sitting in the coffee shop when he came in. That's how I knew he didn't recognise me from when I'd been surveilling Sarah before. I was sitting there, when out of the corner of my eye I saw him walk straight in to the coffee shop. We were discussing and finalising plans. I couldn't believe what I saw. Are we burned?

I looked directly into Pieter's eyes. I had to leave, I told him, because I needed to go to the market. He argued with me, telling me that he'd not finished his coffee yet. I. Have. To. Go. Now. And there he is, asking for five more minutes. Pieter was a great guy, and he was usually really switched-on, but sometimes he could be a little slow to spot even clear cues like that, or notice that a situation had changed.

I grabbed his arm. We've got to go. He downed his coffee. Finally we got outside. He was still clueless until I asked him "What the fuck were you doing? That. Was. The. Fucking. Target." To be fair, it was hilarious how he didn't click on. This was the day before the operation. It was January 10th, and we'd planned the extraction for the 11th. Sarah was due to fly back in to Beirut that day. The father would meet her at the airport and take both her and her daughter to the hotel. At that point, we planned for Sarah to take the child to the hotel toilets as they were checking in. The extraction would happen before they even got to the room.

Now that the father had been in the hotel doing a recce the day before, it was one of those 'he said, she said' situations. Because he'd been tipped off, it seemed clear that he was suspicious about a potentially imminent rescue attempt. I like to think that I was doing enough so that he could never be sure, because he didn't see the metaphorical 'smoking gun' or any actual evidence of our presence.

This was a major security concern. He's doing what I do, I thought. If I were in his situation, damn right I'd be doing a recce of the hotel before going into that situation. I'd want to know in advance what's happening. But with the extraction just hours away, and knowing that he had his vehicles with him outside, I started thinking that I needed more manpower. The whole thing was supposed to go off smoothly, but a bit of extra protection wouldn't go amiss.

Chapter 14 - Quay Decisions

"I don't think you really know for sure what you'll do until it comes down to the moment when you have to make that decision for real." - J.W. Lynne

The operation was set to take place on January 11th. It fitted in nicely with one of my little superstitions. I like seeing double numbers: an 11, 22 or 33. Eleven's particularly good. It's a prime number. It makes me feel like I'm on track. The Stuttgart case finished at 15:15. The Japan case finished on December 13th, on the 13th day of the operation, and we were taxiing down the runway at 13:13. The number 11 would come back up again, but not until later – no spoilers! Perhaps it's just my human brain and how I perceive things, but when I see that kind of repetition of numbers it just feels good and right in some way. When I don't see them, I get a sense that there's something wrong.

Now, though, it was the evening of the 10th. We knew that a bit of extra protection was going to be needed, so Pieter took me to a shady place just outside Beirut. We met with two big burly men under the archway of a bridge in the dark. I explained that I would pay them to stay in our hotel for the night and protect me in case anything happens. Once we're finished, they'd receive a substantial sum of money for doing so. I only had around £2,000 remaining in the budget at this point, and pretty much half of that was going to be spent on this additional protection. Money was going to be particularly tight from now on.

They were stoneheads. It was the best that Pieter could do at short notice. I can't say that I immediately warmed to them or trusted them, but what choice did I have? So they came down to the hotel and spent the whole night partying before bailing on me. They demanded payment at around 9am. I wasn't exactly going to pay them in advance of the mission going down. They started kicking off, saying that we weren't going to pay up, and walked off. Now we were left to finish the mission with no manpower remaining for support. Sarah was due to arrive within an hour, so there wasn't much time to find someone else. It was a real 'shit, what are we going to do now?' moment.

"Okay, I'll fix it." That's pretty much how Pieter used to see things. If there was a problem, he'd remain calm and provide a solution. In this case, it was his own brother who headed down to the hotel so that we'd got someone else in position.

We're just minutes away from Sarah's scheduled arrival time. We're expecting her at 10am. The father picks her up from the airport, but I get a text message. The daughter isn't with him. Apparently she had diarrhoea, and the father is going to drive to Miriata and collect her after dropping Sarah off at the hotel. I didn't know what to think. There were three main possibilities.

The child's father doesn't have the same level of experience of military operations as I do. He's done a recce of the hotel, but maybe he's got some irrational fear that we're going to try to rescue the child from the airport. That doesn't make much sense. I'm pretty sure the place is controlled by Hezbollah, and in any case it's the last place where you could come up with a plan for recovering a child. But then, isn't that the point about irrational fears? They are irrational.

The second possibility is that he's got a sense that something's up, and he's just trying to be unpredictable. In that case, fair play to him I suppose. I can respect someone making a sound tactical decision. I didn't dislike him specifically, or indeed have any feelings about him personally one way or the other. It's much better to keep a clear head and be objective about the job. He was just a target, with no emotional connection on that end. Yes, when it came to Sarah and her daughter, I wanted to get them home because it was the right thing to do – but I needed to make sure that I was calm and rational with the actions I was taking.

Finally, there was the third possibility. There's always the chance that he was in fact telling the truth and that he didn't want to take the child to the airport, with the possibility of waiting around if a flight were delayed, before heading to the hotel. In real life, sometimes these things all blur into one. Maybe the child did indeed feel a bit unwell, but that gave the father an excuse to change plans and keep everyone guessing.

The time ticked on, and it was now past 3pm. We needed to abandon the plan for the day, because our boat had been slapped with a curfew. The problem was that we didn't know when it would be possible to actually carry it out if not today. The biggest fear is that the father will get his security in place, tightening everything up, and we're right back to the same stalemate – leaving Sarah stuck in the hotel. We couldn't have a rescue plan from Breakfast to Breakfast or Dunkin' Donuts, because she'd certainly be followed everywhere she went.

I met up with Sarah outside the hotel room to explain the bad news that we had no choice but to abandon the plan for the day. It would such a shame to have to call the mission off, but it couldn't be helped. Pieter was still in position sitting outside in the car on a side street, ready to effect a quick getaway.

I explained to her that the boat would no longer be able to leave, because it had been slapped with a 15:00 curfew and that an overnight stay had never been part of the plan. Her disappointment and confusion was evident. There's always a denial stage when it comes to grief, and this wasn't far off that. I think she was about to try and persuade me that we should still go anyway, or at least check and challenge all my reasoning, when we were interrupted. She was saying 'yes, but what if I can get her to the toilets…?' but the thought was unfinished, as she received a text message from the child's father. They had arrived in the hotel reception, and he was sitting on the sofa with her having a coffee.

That created a moment of urgency. If the father came upstairs now, he'd see me and the entire mission would be compromised. Sarah had to rush straight down to meet them, and our conversation couldn't be finished. The hotel had a strange layout. On the ground floor, in the reception area, there was effectively a coffee bar open to the public. There were two sets of stairs: one to the left, and one to the right. The stairs on the right went all the way up to the hotel rooms, whilst the stairs on the left went up only as far as the breakfast area. The breakfast area was connected to both sets of stairs, so that it would be possible for someone to walk up the left-hand set of stairs, cross the breakfast area, and then go up the right-hand set of stairs to the hotel rooms. The fire escape was located up the right-hand set of stairs, near the hotel rooms. The toilets were in the breakfast area, which is why the original plan had been for Sarah to take her daughter to the toilets and be rescued from there.

Pieter's brother was still having a coffee in the breakfast area, sitting and waiting for the operation. I was on the right-hand set of stairs, heading down towards the breakfast area. I started to compose a text message to explain that there was no choice in the matter, that the whole operation would have to be abandoned for the day.

They say that real life is stranger than fiction, and the child's diarrhoea once again became relevant to the story. Almost as soon as Sarah saw her daughter, her daughter wanted to be taken to the toilets. Sarah saw it as an opportunity to get the mission to proceed immediately. Whilst I was still trying to find the right words for my text to call the mission off, I received a message from Sarah telling me that she might be able to get to the toilets. If she could, would we be able to proceed with the plan and leave immediately?

I thought for a moment. Literally everything that could be put in place was in position and we didn't have a clue when that was going to be the case again, but the fact was that there was no way we could possibly get the boat out today.

It was a chance, and you should never look a gift horse in the mouth. But if we did manage to rescue them, what would our next move be? Everyone in the country would be looking for us. We can't go ahead. There's just no way. But what if I can get her to the toilets somehow? I don't see how. But then we still have no way to get out of this country till tomorrow morning at 7am. What would we do in the meantime?

In one of the biggest ironies of my life, whilst we were sitting in the bar ready to get on with our escape, the hotel staff sat down for a meeting. They all knew that something was going to go down. Management was making it absolutely clear to their staff that they must not get involved, one way or another. This wasn't their business and they didn't want their hotel to end up being part of a situation like this. Whatever their personal feelings, they were to stay out of it.

No, the answer had to be 'no'. I started to compose a reply, explaining that there's no way we could manage to get a boat out today and that we were going to have to try another time. It was a difficult text to write, knowing that I couldn't offer any alternative plan for any other day. I started typing the reply.

Before I could send my reply, a second text message came in. It was Sarah again. They were now in the toilets and ready to go.

If only this had happened a couple of hours earlier, it would have been perfect.

Chapter 15 -
A few good men

*"Sometimes you have to risk life in order
to live, and gamble death, to sacrifice life"*
- Anthony Liccione

There are 'fuck it' moments in life. They're the times when you've just got to bite the bullet and make a big decision. They're the times when the gambler says "let it ride" after winning big on roulette. They're the times when you know you really shouldn't tell your mate that his girlfriend's shagging his second cousin twice removed, but you tell him anyway. They're the times when you don't really have the cash to buy your dream home, but you take the plunge. Sometimes, big or small, there are times when your instinct screams out at you to throw out the theory and follow your heart. Those are the 'do or die' moments, when you've got a huge decision to make.

Like Kenny Rogers' famous song The Gambler, you gotta know when to walk away and know when to run. But you've also gotta know when to go 'all in' at the poker table, when to make your stand and go for the big win. There's a South African song, which the mercenaries used to sing, using the same tune as The Gambler. It's called "The Heavy", and the plot is pretty much the same – except that it doesn't involve a gambler on a train, but a South African mercenary (or 'heavy') who's in a bar offering advice and stories of the old war in exchange for whisky. The younger generation would sit, listen and learn at the feet of a wizened veteran for the price of a drink. Having told his story, the heavy dies in the best way that he possibly could: peacefully, in his sleep, reminiscing about the good old days.

We used to enjoy sitting around eating a braai and drinking whisky to chill out after a long day of dodging bombs and bullets, and so 'The Heavy' holds a special place in my heart because it captures those times perfectly. That's what I love when it comes to music: songs which tell a story, which transport you to a certain time and place, making you feel like you're a part of that precious moment. In some ways, I imagine myself as having graduated to become the 'heavy' –

by writing this book, in a sense this is my barstool. I'm telling you my stories of the war.

Today was the 11th. I had my superstitions. Everything was aligned, and the operation was sitting right there waiting to happen. If we took the plunge, anything could happen. We'd have to sort out what to do overnight and how to stay safe. We didn't have all the answers, and we couldn't possibly have a comprehensive plan. The decision had to be made. I pushed my fear and doubts to one side and made a decision. There was no way I was going to fail.

Fuck it.

The operation's a go. Go, go...GO!

Pieter's brother went to collect Sarah and her daughter from the toilets, escorting them through the breakfast area. They came back quickly, everything happening in a flash. I stayed, watching the second set of stairs like a hawk. I thought for a split second that I heard footsteps. It was a heart-in-mouth moment: I instantly decided that if anyone walked up those stairs, they'd be going back fucking down them one way or another.

I had to make sure that I kept both sets of stairs covered. In one swift motion, the whole plan came into fruition. Everything moved like clockwork. I moved to open the breakfast area door for them, and then Pieter's brother tapped me on the shoulder as they walked past me towards the other set of stairs heading up to the hotel rooms. I waited for just a second or two to check that nobody was following us, then moved to follow Pieter's brother with Sarah and her daughter.

I was now bringing up the rear and protecting it with the only weapon at my disposal which I kept hidden out of sight. It was a can of CS gas, which Pieter had been able to secure for me at a local market. It felt strange, almost naked, to be going into this kind of action without a gun. How was I supposed to protect myself without a gun? It reminded me of the old maritime security days, when we'd need to make do with whatever we could cobble together if we needed to defend ourselves. What's even worse is that I didn't even know if it fucking worked. For just a split second, the girl from the reception desk caught my eye and flashed a huge smile at me. None of them could or would say a thing, but it was good to know that they weren't going to do anything to cause us a problem. There was a look on all their faces of total shock as if to say 'fucking hell, they're going home right now – during our meeting'. As we walked past, you could have heard a pin drop. They fell into a shocked silence.

The door closed behind me as we got into the fire escape. It was a rickety old thing, which wouldn't have passed modern health and safety regulations in the United Kingdom to say the least. We had to descend the black, rusting old spiral staircase outside on the fire escape in order to get down. With four of us going down the stairs, it was swaying from side to side a little. Of all the things which could possibly go wrong, I hadn't considered until now the possibility of the staircase collapsing on us. Fortunately it was only a little rocking motion, and the metal bolts held for us to walk down. Of all the things I'd expected to be nervous about, this certainly wasn't one of them.

Pieter was waiting at the bottom of the stairs, ushering everyone into the Porsche Cayenne which we'd rented. Meanwhile, knowing that there were no security cameras, Pieter's brother walked off quickly in the opposite direction. He could blend seamlessly into the background, fucking off out of there as quickly as possible and staying well out of any possible investigation. Everything had to be done quickly. Sarah and her daughter were told to keep their heads well down. I'd got a brief which I'd used for protecting clients in Iraq and Afghanistan, which I quickly repurposed to explain that they needed not to be visible from any windows. If he had his people outside, we didn't want them to see them in the back of that car. We'd chosen a vehicle which made that fairly easy to achieve.

This time, unlike in Stuttgart, I didn't have an alternative vehicle ready to change into. I didn't need one. There are fewer CCTV cameras in Byblos, so I was far less concerned about the vehicle being tracked within minutes. The intention this time had been for us to be onto a boat within five minutes of being in the car, so changing cars would have been an unnecessary hurdle. Up to this point, the plan had worked as efficiently as could have possibly been imagined. Now, though, we faced a lengthy wait. We hadn't planned on enacting the rescue fifteen hours before we could get to the boat, but that's the way it had panned out. Now we had a lot of time to kill without putting ourselves into any more danger than necessary.

First, though, we had to take our immediate security into account. We had to put some distance between us and the hotel as quickly as possible. As we came to the junction, we turned in the opposite direction to the hotel. I could just about see into the hotel, craning my neck behind me at a five-o-clock angle. I saw enough to be able to see the father still sitting there, the luggage next to him, waiting for Sarah and her daughter to come back out of the toilet. It was the first, and hopefully only, time in my life when I was grateful for a child having diarrhoea. That had probably bought us a few extra minutes before anything started to seem suspicious. I told Pieter to drive up into the hills, which he did. That would give me some time to be able to formulate another plan whilst on the run.

One of the surprising things about this whole rescue was just how many things that one bout of diarrhoea affected, both good and bad. It had delayed the mission, causing us to miss our boat. Then it had bought us some vital time. Now, it rather ruled out any plan of us trying to find some secluded spot to hide away overnight and sleep in the car. Lebanon's a small country, and as we'd seen out in Miriata, there are military checkpoints. No way could I reasonably drive around for the next fifteen hours without a serious risk of being pulled over.

There was only one thing for it. I turned to Pieter, informing him that we needed a fucking safe house. Now. In the meantime, I made a quick phone call to Mick and another one to Chris. I informed Mick that we've got them, but that there were unspecified problems causing delay. No need to risk explaining what the problems actually were. As for Chris, I made it clear that he needed to be at the co-ordinates I'd given him at 7.30am on the dot. The next logistical step was to make sure that the yacht owner would be able to be in place in international waters. We'd had to change the timings, and it would be an absolute disaster if the rhib were to find itself stranded in the middle of the Mediterranean. Everyone now knew exactly what needed to happen, and there could be no further comms with anyone until 7am the next day. All of the pieces were in place on the chessboard, and any further chatter would just be a security risk. The burner phone got fucking ditched. We needed to disappear.

Half of Lebanon would likely be looking for us within minutes. If the police weren't launching a large-scale hunt, the father's Hezbollah terrorist mates certainly would be. We'd headed up for the hills, buying ourselves some time.

Pieter was resigned to the only solution that he could think of. He was going to offer us his house, at great personal risk, with all the warmth and hospitality you'd expect of a Lebanese Christian. His house just happened to be in this direction. He'd clearly anticipated what I was going to ask, and had already driven us in the direction of his house. We didn't even need to turn around. The speed at which everything happened was just so smooth, as though I was watching it replay on fast-forward. Decisions were being taken on a second-by-second basis. Strange how at one point the rescue was getting absolutely nowhere for a number of months, but now it barely went a minute without something happening.

I hesitated for a moment, or at least I wanted to hesitate. The level of risk that this would cause Pieter and his family was significant. I couldn't for the life of me think of another reasonable option, so I agreed. They needed, though, to take their family to stay somewhere else that night. If any shit went down, I didn't want Pieter's family to be quite literally caught in the crossfire. We'd just go to sleep and lock the place down.

I told Pieter to take the Porsche Cayenne while we would lock his house down all night. We arrived, and the process of us moving in and them moving out happened as quickly as possible. The last thing we wanted was to be seen acting suspiciously around Pieter's house. We arranged with Pieter that he would pick us up at 7am, on the dot. Until then, of course, no communication would be possible.

Pieter lived in a small one-bedroom apartment, no bigger than a studio flat. I looked around. It had no back door, meaning that if anyone came in the front door there was no way of making a run for it out of the back. I started to scan the apartment, my military training kicking in as I considered the tactical situation of trying to defend it. Frankly, it wasn't good. I needed to hope that nobody had tracked us here. The car clearly hadn't been followed, at least. As Pieter drove off with his wife and child in tow, the longest night of my life had just begun.

Chapter 16 -
Where angels fear to tread

"Sleep is such a luxury, which I can't afford" -
Robin Sikarwar

Sarah and her daughter stayed in the back bedroom, as far away as possible from the front of the apartment. Bless the child, she was so good and so quiet. If there had been lots of noise and crying, it might have jeopardised everything, but there wasn't a peep out of her all night.

Sarah had her iPhone with her. Fuck! iPhones are so easily tracked, because even if you switch them off there's still a battery inside. I could take the battery out of a burner phone without much difficulty, but if you want to start messing around with the battery in an iPhone you're probably going to need a PhD in Apple or something. I searched frantically for tin foil and wrapped it up in as much foil as I possibly could. Hopefully that would be enough to jam the signal if anyone was able to find Sarah's number and try to trace the phone that way.

I sat in the front, guarding the only entrance. If someone came through that door, we would have no escape. My paranoia had been growing, acting in this unfamiliar country in unfamiliar ways, but this night was something like I'd never experienced before. There was a shop just next door to the apartment, so there were people walking past during the late afternoon and evening. Every footstep I heard could be the authorities, or terrorists. I stayed in a constant state of readiness, refusing to drift off. The can of CS gas was my only weapon, so my best chance would be the element of surprise. If someone came through that door, they'd be getting it first and questions would only be asked later.

My mind started to turn to every threat, knowing that there was absolutely nothing I could do to control anything until the morning. Every second that went by was a second closer to safety.

I had to trust Pieter. I had to trust that he wasn't going to get captured, or do anything stupid that could give us away. I had to trust that he wouldn't give us up if a reward was put out. I had to trust that he wasn't going to talk to anyone. Most of all, I had to trust that he was actually going to come back in the morning. We'd gone to his house, and it was in a safe enough area, but we'd not put much distance between us and the site of the extraction. If any kind of search operation was underway, it'd be round here.

More footsteps.

I gripped the can of CS gas tightly, body poised and alert, ready to spring up at a split-second's notice.

The footsteps subsided.

I couldn't exactly relax, but the imminent threat had subsided. I wasn't capable of breathing a sigh of relief, or capable of calming down. I started going through in my mind how we could possibly be caught.

What would happen if we were caught? Would I end up languishing in a Lebanese jail on trumped-up charges for the next two decades? Or would I be killed outright either by terrorists or as I fought to escape and protect Sarah and her daughter? Neither thought appealed to me. Either could happen, right this second.

Another set of footsteps. Behind the frosted glass of the door, I could just about make out the silhouette of a human being. Man or woman, I couldn't tell. Were they trying to peer in through the window? Could they see anything if they did?

I heard the footsteps again, this time walking away.

What if Pieter doesn't return at 7am? How can we get to the boat for 7.30am in that case? We've got problems if that happens. I need a plan. My mind was racing, trying to navigate my way through the maze of possibilities.

And again, footsteps. I tensed up once more, but they went straight past. Probably a customer at the shop, but as my thoughts started to return to security and operational matters, I was interrupted by more footsteps. I became like a coiled spring, listening intently through my good ear, then it was back to my thoughts.

Shit, I thought. Are Sarah and her daughter okay? I hadn't checked on them for a couple of hours. I'd be losing track of time completely if it weren't for the clock on the wall. I went to check on them. Yes, they were fine – or at least as fine as they could be under the circumstances. All I could say was to reassure them that we were going to make it, that we'd be out of Lebanon in the morning.

I could give any kind of assurances and make all sorts of comforting remarks, but at the end of the day it was all outside my control. That's what really drove the paranoia. It was the knowledge that there was nothing I could do, that I couldn't change anything.

This time I hear a car pull up outside, before more footsteps. I see another shadowy silhouette outside the door. Were they trying to look in? I started to wonder, idly, if I might be going mad. They went away, and then back again a couple of minutes later. I heard the car drive off. Must have been another shop customer.

What would I do in the event that Pieter didn't turn up? I wondered about phoning for a taxi. Risky, not knowing the scale of any operation to track us, and in any case what location would I give? My destination was a cliff and pile of rocks. But if it worked, it had the advantage of being quick. I didn't like the plan. It was leaving far too much to chance.

My heart was still pounding as yet another set of footsteps went by outside. Was this it? Was I finally about to hear the dreaded knock on the door, or the terrifyingly loud crack of someone breaking it down by force? Again, there was nothing to worry about.

By now the daughter was asleep. I suspected that Sarah was even managing to get a little sleep. She was fearful but hopeful, and we never talked about the worst-case scenario. Why should we?

I looked at the clock. It was 2am, just five hours before Pieter was due to pick us up. My next concern was about checkpoints and roadblocks. Would any of those be in place? They were very common in Lebanon at the best of times, but if any search was underway then it could be even worse.

Why was I still hearing footsteps, even at this time? Don't they ever stop? Fortunately, the Mediterranean apartments aren't like our houses with windows that can easily be looked through. In Lebanon, just like you'd find in Southern Spain or Italy, there's frosted glass windows high up with bars on the outside. Nobody would be able to see in, surely, so long as we kept the lights off. The lack of an alternative escape route really played on my mind. Had this culture never heard of health and safety?

I started to wonder whether something was perhaps going on outside. After all, the later it got, the less need there would be for the general public to be roaming the streets. From that moment, the can of CS gas didn't leave my hand. If anyone came through that door, I was ready to fight for my life.

What were the risks? It was going dark already when we arrived, so the risk of having been seen by neighbours – or the neighbours putting two and two together then shopping us to the authorities – was low. If we had been seen, then yes it would be a major problem. But I was pretty sure I was safe on that score – or was I? What if I was wrong? I started to second-guess myself as I heard more footsteps and held on to the can of CS gas even tighter.

The second huge potential risk was if anyone connected me to Pieter. They might figure out that I was using Pieter's house as a safe house, or simply come here looking for Pieter and accidentally find me with the mother and child. This really was not the ideal situation. I am no fan of being reliant upon luck.

Was I being overly paranoid? I was certainly being paranoid, but the fears seemed well-placed to me. It's only paranoia if the things you're scared of aren't realistic, plausible or logical. The concern here was genuine, not that I could let on to Sarah about that.

The time dragged on, hour by hour. It felt awful, especially when I'd hear cars pulling up outside or see the silhouette of someone, not quite knowing whether they might be trying to peer through the window. I assumed the worst, that they were looking for us. And if they came through that door, I knew it was all over.

Lack of sleep breeds paranoia. The fear was gripping me, largely because we weren't in a true action situation to take my mind off things. This was a 13-hour wait. Possibly I drifted off for half an hour. I jolted myself upright. This would not do! If I'd fallen asleep on duty in the Army I'd have been up on a charge, and rightly so. Falling asleep in the Army means a charge, but falling asleep here and now could get me killed. I needed to stay awake, even though I wanted to sleep. I wanted to sleep, but I probably wouldn't have got much decent sleep if I'd tried. Would it be irresponsible of me to take a couple of hours' nap? Yes. But there was a gruelling day ahead, and I didn't want to be running on empty.

The minutes ticked by, and then the hours, footsteps and noises heightening my sense of paranoia once more. My life was flashing before my eyes. I knew that I had to conquer the fear, harness the fear even, and use it for the mission.

What other options did I have? I could hijack a car if Pieter didn't turn up. Lebanese cars are modern enough, so hotwiring would be out.

We'd literally have to steal it in the street, Grand Theft Auto style, but getting Sarah and her daughter into the vehicle would mean absolute precision would be required.

By now it was 5am. Just a couple of hours more until Pieter was due to arrive.

What if? Those are the two hardest words in the English language. But I was determined to avoid the four saddest words: 'it might have been'. I was not one for leaving any stone unturned in my pursuit of a mission. Like the footballer who is described as having 'laid it on the line' or 'left it all on the pitch', I was always going to throw everything at this. I work hard and I play hard. That's how life should be lived.

6.30am, and it was time to make sure that Sarah and her daughter are up. They needed to eat something, with a long and potentially turbulent sea crossing ahead. They're awake, and I get the sense that Sarah has been awake for some time.

By 6.55am, everyone was ready to leave.

The clock turned over to 7am. Pieter hadn't turned up. The fear reached a whole new level as I tried to work out how I was going to get out of this one.

7.01am, and I was starting to truly panic. What had gone wrong? Which option should I choose for trying to rescue something from this shitshow? I was a man on the run. My options were limited, and only long shots remained at this stage.

Where the fuck had Pieter got to? My thoughts and emotions were now in overdrive.

7.02am. A car pulled up outside. I heard footsteps, and a key turning in the door. It must be Pieter, I thought. And it was. There was a huge smile on his face. He was so relaxed it was unbelievable, oblivious to the agony I'd endured overnight and especially in the last two minutes. Why hadn't he been on time?

You bastard, I thought, but I only said "let's get out of here now".

Chapter 17 -
And on this rock

"I tell you that you are Peter, and on this rock I will build my church" - Matthew 16:18, The Bible, New International Version

What's it like out there? That's the first, and only, question that I wanted Pieter to answer. He told me to relax, not to worry. He assured me that it'd be alright, that we'd get down there now. I wasn't particularly seeking reassurance. I wanted to know the tactical situation. Were there any police checkpoints? Is there a manhunt underway? Pieter didn't say very much. I got the impression that he genuinely didn't think there was anything to worry about, but it's often difficult to tell. If he were any more laid back, he'd be comatose.

We moved straight to the vehicle. There wasn't much time to spare. The boat couldn't leave the harbour until 7am, so we'd arranged to meet by 7.30. We expected it to take the rhib just under half an hour to get into position. I phoned at 7.08, just as the car was setting off, using my final burner phone for the call. We still had Sarah's phone of course, but because it was connected to us, we didn't intend to turn that on until we arrived back in Cyprus.

"Come on, hurry up!" I wasn't particularly expecting to hear those words from Chris, but apparently the journey had been much quicker than planned. It was more difficult to keep the boat steady around the rocks than he'd expected. It was bouncing around. Now the concern was whether the boat was going to breach its hull. We were going as fast as we could without risking being stopped by police. The drive down to the drop-off point was as uneventful as it could possibly be. I was in the front with Pieter, whilst Sarah and her kid were ducking down and hiding from sight in the back.

When we reached the cliff, however, something was wrong. We approached the coast only to see a big black SUV. A long-haired Lebanese man wearing a sharp suit and sunglasses was standing outside, on the phone as we approached. My first thought was that we must have been caught, but then why was there only one person there? Surely Chris would have told me if there was anyone down on the beach, and why would someone be acting alone when we're this close to a boat? It really didn't make much sense. He must be someone in government, but who is he and what exactly is he doing there?

It was far too late to call the operation off now. We had to keep going. Thoughts might have been racing through my mind. There was only one single-minded determination though: this cunt is not going to stop me getting on that boat. We got out of the vehicle at the top of the cliff. I decided to find out some information in the most basic, obvious way possible.

"Good morning!", I confidently called out. It's never clear which language to use when you're in Lebanon. The official language is Arabic, but as a remnant of the old colonial days French is often spoken. English is also common, particularly amongst the younger generation. In a more practical sense, I speak English. I only speak a little Arabic, which I've picked up over the years.

A friendly greeting was an easy way to precipitate any conflict which might arise. It became difficult for him to completely ignore our presence, even if he turned out to be a government official. I also had a vague notion that if we acted normal and confident, we might just seem like we were a family heading out for a fishing trip by boat. A bit unlikely, perhaps, but then the truth was pretty far-fetched too.

The adrenaline was pulsing through my veins as we walked past him. I was thinking that if he tried to stop us boarding the boat, he's going to end up in the drink. We came down the steps only to see an old man there, fishing, where the boat was rocking around. I wondered whether it was possible that the suit-wearing SUV man could be the old man's son. The boat is still bounding off the rocks on both sides. The guys throw a rope and we pull it in, Sarah helping me to pull it towards shore. House gets off the boat whilst Chris is piloting it, trying to control it with the engines. I pass the kid to House. He takes the kid onto the boat and then Sarah gets on. I throw my day sack onto the boat, then turn around to shake Pieter's hand and say my goodbyes.

Saying goodbye to Pieter on the rocks was one of the most poignant moments of my life. Over the last few weeks, he had truly been my rock. I've changed everyone's names to protect their real identity, but I chose the name Pieter because in the Bible Jesus describes Peter as his 'rock': I can't think of any better way to honour Pieter than to choose that name for him. He was solid, reliable, dependable and calm. I can't remember the exact words that we used, but the communication between us will forever be etched into my brain. He reached around his neck and removed a long golden chain with a cross on it, symbolic of his strong Christian faith. He reached over to me and placed the cross around my neck.

It was a symbolic gesture. It said 'thank you', though in reality I was thanking him for the support that he'd given to my mission. It said 'stay safe', an odd allusion to the custom since time immemorial of sailors having some keepsake whilst on a dangerous journey. Most of all, though, it said something about his Christian faith. It said that he was thinking of me, that he was praying for protection over everyone on the boat, and that he had faith we would be kept safe. Of everyone connected with this mission, Pieter had been the calmest. He had a simple, almost childlike confidence that we would succeed – and gave up his own home to show us hospitality. To this day, I regret that (as with all missions) I couldn't keep in contact with Pieter afterwards. I'm sure that Oskar will have informed him of the outcome. As I'm writing these words, I'm staring at that cross hanging up in front of me. I've kept it as a reminder. A reminder that we got home safely, a reminder of Pieter, and a reminder of the mission I'm most proud of.

It was an emotional moment. I don't do emotions most of the time, but something about that moment got to me. Pieter reached out and gave me a hug, wishing me all the best. I thanked him for his help and boarded the boat.

As we set off, we tried to reverse back out. The boat was bobbing and weaving around everywhere. We had to get far enough away from the rocks so that we could spin the boat around and gun it. We were getting thrown around everywhere. The back of the boat was starting to come apart, which was a little concerning to say the least when we'd got so far to travel.

Twelve miles. Twelve nautical miles. That's the same as around fourteen miles inland. That's how far we needed to travel to get into international waters and out of Lebanese jurisdiction. The first step in the journey was to get beyond that 12-mile limit. We weren't going to slow down one iota until the moment we'd crossed that invisible boundary in the sea. We saw nothing: nothing with our eyes, nothing on the radar. It was quiet out there, apart from the roar of the sea and the waves splashing over the boat. Why was this so easy?

As the adrenaline started to wear off, with no imminent threat other than the ever-present concern that the boat could fall apart around us, I remembered that I was suffering from seasickness. There's something of a literary tradition where authors make their seafaring characters suffer from seasickness to show their fallibility. C.S. Forester afflicted the famous Hornblower with it – having his hero ridiculed as a young officer as the 'sailor who was seasick in Spithead'.

Sarah had taken a tablet, as had her daughter. They were as safe and sound as possible, wearing life vests and blankets. I couldn't risk taking a seasickness tablet myself because I needed to be fully alert, and those tablets do have a habit of causing serious drowsiness. I'd managed to cope on bigger boats when doing marine security operations, but crossing the Mediterranean on a 6.4 metre rhib was something else altogether. I was soon leaning over the side, feeling as ill as fuck and trying to avoid the humiliation of throwing up all over the place. I'm not sure that would have exactly inspired Sarah to have much confidence in me.

I'd not planned to be on this boat at all. My original plan had been to see Sarah and her daughter safely onto the boat, then fly out through Beirut airport. The delay in getting out of there, coupled with the questions that had been asked of me at immigration, made that route seem particularly risky. I've since managed to find out, on the grapevine through certain covert but reliable channels, that I'm considered a 'person of interest' by the Lebanese authorities for my role in this rescue mission. I'd clearly made the right decision.

For once, the plan was actually running smoothly. There was only one problem. When we got onto the boat, we found out that House hadn't turned on the cameras that we'd rigged up to make sure that everything was safe. We always do that to provide evidence of the job that we've done, to show that we've done everything possible to protect our client. Still, by his standards it was a minor fuck-up. This one didn't threaten the mission itself.

I still couldn't get my head around why nobody was chasing us. Yes, the boat had a tuna fishing licence for the day, but why wasn't anyone wondering why this boat was shooting out to sea at breakneck speed? The whole thing seemed really surreal at the time, especially after we'd passed the twelve-mile limit. I didn't know what to think: was it the lull in the battle, or was the battle over? I didn't know whether I should be relaxed or still on full alert. That confusion continued for quite some time. A crossing of over a hundred miles seems to take forever, especially when there's a constant non-specific feeling of danger. Hour after hour of seeing nothing but sea, waiting for the moment when we could make the transfer to the yacht and evade any questions at customs by avoiding them altogether.

We kept trying to raise the yacht on the radio. Nothing was coming through. Fucking hell, I thought, I hope he's there. We were completely reliant on him being there. The frustration from waiting kept growing as it felt like such slow progress, just hoping that the boat would hold together. Still nothing. Silence on the comms.

Finally, we heard one word amidst all the static. "Viking…"

That single word was everything we needed to hear. When we'd registered the boat, we'd called it Viking. The yacht was out there, trying to reach us just as much as we were trying to reach them. I didn't give a stuff really what they were saying. The closer we got, the better comms would get. At least we knew that they were out there now, and they probably knew that we were on our way. They must have heard our message, or at least part of it.

The comms did indeed start to improve. We reported that we were in the middle of the Med, on our way home, still in international waters but soon to cross over into Cypriot waters. I was still trying everything to hold that frame together. I couldn't see it lasting all the way back. We started to contemplate scuttling the boat.

No, said the mafia boss emphatically. He explained that there was a loose end: our boat had left Lebanon without telling the authorities we were going anywhere. Why had we headed to Cyprus? Having a battered boat would provide the perfect explanation. We were out fishing for tuna in the Med, when we hit some seriously choppy waters. The frame of the boat gave way, and we didn't think we'd make it back to Beirut. Instead, we had no choice but to head for Cyprus. That was the safest place to go. We'd get a bollocking from immigration and customs no doubt, but they wouldn't do anything to us. How could they? They have eyes. They could see for themselves that the boat was battered and had a frame that was falling apart. We'd acted in an emergency situation, or Chris and House had.

The yacht's owners were doing this for the sake of humanity, rather than for monetary reward. In fact they absolutely refused to take a penny more than was strictly necessary to pay for their fuel and out-of-pocket expenses. That was a huge blessing, because we didn't have the money in the budget to pay for it. Such generosity is not a character trait that you would traditionally associate with mafia, but even with the Sicilian lot there was that incredibly strong sense of family. It was clear just how much they were moved by Sarah's plight. The contrast between them and the dodgy Lebanese characters hanging around that marina on the other side of the Med was stark: one was motivated by money, the other by sympathy and caring for family. During the Lebanon operation I developed a close relationship with the Cypriot guys, and even after the mission was complete we used to meet up regularly in the marina for food and drinks.

We made our final approach to the yacht, with huge smiles of elation and relief all around. Everyone was delighted. This was the moment that we knew we'd done it. We were finally on the home stretch. They threw ropes out, pulled us in and got Sarah and her daughter straight over. We all followed, clambering up onto the rather luxurious yacht – often used for tourist day-cruises.

A distinctive smell wafted through the air: fish cooking on charcoal. Whilst they'd been waiting for us, the yacht had got their crew to do a bit of fishing – and they were now barbecuing a feast. In true Greek mezze-style, various salads and freshly-caught fish were being served. This was proper hospitality, another reminder that for the crew of the yacht working on this mission, this was more than just a job. There's something special about an on-deck barbecue of fish that had come out of the water less than an hour earlier, an experience which I'd have enjoyed even more if I hadn't just been through hell over the previous 24 hours.

It was all about rescuing a 4-year-old little girl. Everyone else was so hungry, having been open to the waves and eaten nothing for many hours. I might have been hungry, if it weren't for the seasickness. I struggled to eat anything. Within minutes we'd gone from a life-or-death situation to being looked after as though we were on a cruise liner. Many things had been truly surreal about this whole mission, but this was the final major surprise to me.

The next challenge was for us to get into Cyprus without being questioned. The pressure was already off to an extent because even if they did question us, we'd still be in Cyprus. They were hardly going to send us back to Lebanon. The whole thing would be messy. We'd rather avoid lots of questions (and a potential temporary arrest) whilst they figured out what the fuck was going on and that we'd not actually done anything illegal, but it wouldn't matter.

Once we were well into Cypriot waters and close enough to the shore that we had reasonable confidence the rhib would actually make it back in one piece, we untied it. Chris, House, and a tapestry of excuses all boarded the boat and made their way back to Larnaca.

We headed for the marina instead of the harbour. As we docked, I headed inside with Sarah and her daughter. We needed to wait another five minutes whilst the boat's crew double-checked that nobody was around. Once we had assurances that the coast was clear, we got off the boat.

Epilogue

Tourists walk up and down the boardwalk all the time. Within seconds of leaving the boat, we looked just like any other tourists who are there. We'd made landfall in Cyprus. We were finally safe. Nothing could have gone any smoother, but the only reason it went so smoothly was the planning that had gone into it.

We walked down the marina, headed towards my car, and then we were gone. The hotel was only a 10-minute drive away, and the look on Sarah's face was priceless. Every concern and worry that had been plaguing her for so many months had just melted away at once. I pulled the car up to the hotel. Everyone was there. Oskar had flown his wife, sons and assorted family members out to be there to greet Sarah. They had a photographer present – whether from the Norwegian press or a member of the family, I didn't know. They'd got themselves a private area on the ground floor of the hotel, with nobody else around. There were hugs and kisses, smiles and laughter – and a few tears of joy or even just relief.

It was a private matter, and my job is to be the angel in the shadows. I'm not in this for the glory, or the thanks, just to actually do the job and rescue kids from tough situations. To do that job properly, I need to keep myself hidden away from view as much as possible. This party wasn't about me. It was about Sarah, her child, and them being back safely. It was about a family reunion, a joyous occasion but one that I shouldn't be around to share. I quietly headed back out to my car and drove off, drifting silently away back into the same shadows from which I'd come.

There were loose ends to tie up, as there often are: people to pay, and they were straight onto the next plane out of Cyprus. The boat needed to be sold to bring some of the cash back in. I simply headed off home and left them to it. The job was done, that's all that mattered. Yes, I had some admin to do later – and I met up with Mick, shaking his hand, before going back to my family. There was no real celebration from us, just the satisfaction of a successful and important job.

Everything went straight back to normal, at least on the surface. That's the problem though: what is 'normal'? By this point I'd been working in military operations of one form or another for roughly two decades. It was clear that it was taking a toll on my physical health, my mental health, and my family life. There's so much that I've learned since then, being able to put everything into a sense of perspective. Having lived in this environment for so long, I've never really known what 'normal' means to most people. Coming back to a civilian lifestyle is a culture shock beyond anything that most people could possibly imagine. If you've never been in that kind of action, you don't have a point of reference to be able to make any comparisons.

The biggest problem with leaving with the Army is that you haven't the faintest idea of how to live as a civilian. I didn't know the first thing about credit scores, personal finances or anything else. Most people gradually develop the simple skills of running their own lives over a period of time, maybe as they go off to university with plenty of support, but for me it was all a total shock. It was easier to adapt from being a 16-year-old boy to becoming a soldier, than adapting from being a soldier to civilian life.

Strangely, the Army is quite sheltered and insular in that way. I suppose it's because the most basic civilian life skills just aren't part of the job description when you're fighting for your country. The Army will make you, but what it creates is just a carbon-copy of a soldier ready-made for a military career. It won't create a well-rounded human being able to cope with civilian life. The private military contracting world doesn't really help with that: you don't get a sense of a normal civilian life, and phrases like "work-life balance" are utterly meaningless. We've been taught how to go to war and to give our life for the greater cause. That's permanently etched into who we are. *The saddest part is this: we were taught how to die, but we were never taught how to live.*

Have you ever wondered why one out of every ten prisoners in the UK is ex-military? That's why. *Adjusting to normal civilian life is terrifying.*

Have you ever wondered why we have more than 50 ex-service personnel commit suicide every year (and those are just the ones we know about)? That's why. *Adjusting to normal civilian life is terrifying.*

Have you ever wondered why 6,000 of our veterans are homeless, sleeping on the streets? That's why. *Adjusting to normal civilian life is terrifying.*

Was I messed up by it? Yeah, too right I was. I know what it's like to be homeless. I'm one of the lucky ones though. I've got a sense of purpose. I know what I'm supposed to be doing with my life and that's rescuing kidnapped kids. Nobody can take that new sense of identity from me. I'm also one of the lucky ones because I've got a loving, supportive wife and kids. Not everyone has that.

I'm not saying any of this as a sob-story. That's not what we do. I'm saying it because society needs to wake up and smell the fucking coffee about what's happening to those who've risked their lives for this country. They deserve more respect and support than they've received, so yeah, I am going to shout from the rooftops about it. If I can be vulnerable, telling you the truth with warts and all, maybe it'll help other people to understand that they're not alone – and maybe, just maybe, someone in government will finally sit up and take notice.

The first thing to hit me, when coming back from Lebanon, was the paranoia. I've grown used to dealing with it now, but back then it was new to me. It lingered for months afterwards. I was fearing reprisals from Lebanon. I didn't know whether that would be the father sending henchmen to take revenge on me, or maybe even the Lebanese equivalent of MI6 coming to have a few 'quiet' words with me. For months, I tried my best to keep the worries hidden from my missus. There was no need to spook her too. We'd be out shopping and I'd have a sense of being followed, so I'd take a different turning and give some random vehicle the slip. She'd tell me "you've missed your turn", as though I'd not been concentrating on the road.

I'd see someone vaguely Lebanese-looking and have that moment of wondering 'who the hell are you?'. I'd do counter-surveillance, checking my car for tracking devices. I would ask myself how I would approach it if I were the person doing surveillance on my house. I went to all the locations from which it would be possible to watch it without easily being detected, to make sure that there wasn't in fact anyone there. I'd be literally walking up and down those roads, looking inside cars. It would take months before I was finally able to come to peace with it all, and even then there was some residual anxiety for a while.

After a few months, the paranoia gradually started to wear off. I started to understand how irrational it actually was. But the physical and mental scars of constant warfare remain to this day, though I've grown to know and understand them far better than I ever did before. Soldiers who've seen significant action often suffer from post-traumatic stress disorder (PTSD). The same goes for private military contractors, who have often seen far more in the way of actual fighting than the soldiers themselves. That's a simple consequence of the U.S. Army's decision to outsource its casualties to private firms.

Imagine, though, that you're struggling – either in the Army or working for a private company. They have mental health check-box exercises. After an action, they'll send someone out to ask you how you're feeling and to check that you're fit for duty. All they're doing in truth is covering their own arses. They don't want to get sued. Everybody knows that if you admit to struggling at all with your mental health, the supply of work is going to dry up. So people suck it up, forget the horrors that they've seen and experienced, and go through the same things again the following day. In military contracting, you're paid to carry out a particular task. If you get a builder in to your house to construct an extension, you don't expect to have an enduring duty of care towards the builder. You get the job done, you pay for the job, and then the builder clears off never to be seen again.

The world of military contracting works in a very similar way: they pay you for a job and you do that job. If you happen to have a cold or the flu, you suck it up and go out to work anyway. What are you going to do? Spend a day in some wilderness somewhere near Lashkar Gah sitting on your arse feeling sorry for yourself and earning no cash whatsoever? You wouldn't spend a day in that environment unless you were getting paid to be there. So you turn up and you do your job, whatever the state of your physical or mental health. That's the reality of the situation. There's a veneer of caring, but scratch the surface and all they see is dollar signs. That's what a military contractor means to the companies they're working for.

The stigma around mental health issues is still there in the private contracting world. Whether or not it's the same in the Army is another matter: it certainly was when I was a soldier, but times have changed a lot since then. Today, I can be a bit more open and honest. There's no reason that I can't (and I'm writing under a pseudonym anyway) admit that my emotions are pretty fucked up, and that I've started therapy to help me through a lot of things. I believe therapy makes a difference, but a lot of it is also force of character. I'm determined never to let the things that have happened to me, the things I've seen, destroy me.

During a mission the adrenaline is pumping. Most people understand that, because we've all had those moments of fight-or-flight responses to situations. The difference is the intensity. Imagine that isn't just a single moment, but it's constant life-threatening moments throughout the day. The adrenaline is always there, for hour after hour, exhausting you in ways that you'd never even begun to think about. You get back to base, fall asleep, and then you're back up the next day to do the same thing again.

The physical toll that it takes is staggering. If you've ever seen "before and after" photos of fresh-faced soldiers going off to war, then coming back a year or two later looking wizened and haggard, wiry as hell, it's because of that sustained pressure over a long period of time. Whilst you're going through it, you don't recognise what's happening. It's only later, looking back, that it's easy to perceive the real levels of stress that you were under.

For me, the most demanding part of the job emotionally was a day-to-day one, being the 'eyes and ears' of a convoy as the lead vehicle when I was doing military contracting. I needed to be able to see any danger as soon as it presented itself. It was a constant vigilance, to the point that I'd almost be able to see a coke can 150 metres away on the side of the road. Everything would be happening so quickly, especially when you're zipping down Route Irish at speeds of over a hundred miles an hour.

That focus creates a hypersensitivity. I'd have a list created inside my head so that I could quickly update everyone in the convoy and let them also put eyes and ears on any potential threat, whether it turned out to be real – or just a coke can. The narrative would be quick: "I need guns facing left side. Potential threat...", together with any further information that's required.

Eventually, once back to base and to safety, the adrenaline wears off. I'd lie down, curled up in a ball, almost comatose from the absolute exhaustion of everything. The lads used to take the piss out of me for it, though all in good fun.

With child rescue, it's different. There's a loneliness which cuts deep. I'll be away on a job for weeks or months at a time. That means taking myself away from my own children in order to rescue someone else's child. I don't really know, for sure, whether I'll ever see my own kids again when I'm away. I can't pick up the phone to talk to them because of OpSEC (operational security). A single phone call could potentially endanger my life, or even theirs. The Channel 4 television programme Hunted features people trying to win a share of a £100,000 jackpot. All they must do is disappear for 30 days, evading security experts trying to catch them. It's a one-off, for just a few weeks, and they're never actually in any real danger. Yet time after time, the show's contestants take risks and contact their close family members – often resulting in them being captured.

Human beings aren't really designed to be away from our loved ones for an extended period of time without any contact. Honestly, after a while it fucks me up when I'm on a mission. I'm on my own, having to think my own thoughts and fight my own demons with no human contact. My daughter, who isn't old enough to understand, thinks that I live and work in an airport. I've sacrificed Christmas, birthdays and so many memorable milestones in my children's development. My wife understands, at least as much as it's humanly possible to understand. She's supportive and caring, and I wouldn't be able to do this kind of work if she weren't. She puts up with a lot, for which I'm so thankful. I know my teenage son supports the principle of what I do, and he thinks it's pretty cool, but the details of how it's affected me would be a shock to him. Worst of all, I never truly understood until quite recently how different all this is. To me, it was just normal – an unremarkable way of life.

I felt I was just like any other professional. If you flip burgers for five months, you're going to be good at flipping burgers. If you sweep the floors, you're going to learn to be good at using a broom. I was just good at something different, which I'd learned to do: fighting, and protecting people.

That mindset was wrong. If I tell people that I work in security, the first thing they'll imagine is some security guard at ASDA trying to prevent shoplifting. I'd always get people asking me when I'm going away and when I'm coming back. They never twigged that there was always a good chance I'd never be coming back. They don't get any idea of the level of danger I encounter on an almost daily basis. We're playing with fire continuously, but almost nobody knows it. So why do I do it? Why do I keep putting myself into danger?

As I ask myself that question, my mind goes back to Afghanistan in around 2011 or 2012. I saw something which I didn't understand at the time. I'm glad I didn't, because there was nothing I could have done. More likely than not, I'd have got myself killed. I saw a number of white girls being taken out of a building, in single file, and led onto a bus. It was incongruous, because it's not something you'd normally expect to see in Afghanistan. One of the girls looked at me, straight in the eye, saying nothing. There was a deep sadness in her eyes, at least the way I remember it. The human memory is a strange thing: we subconsciously reinterpret and re-evaluate our experiences based upon new information as it comes in. It was only perhaps a year or so later, replaying the incident in my mind, that I realised these girls were victims of sex trafficking. Although I was armed, there was only one of me. If I'd foolishly tried to rescue them, I'd have been outnumbered and killed by their captors. What could I possibly have done, even if by some freak chance I'd managed to rescue them, in the middle of a hostile country ravaged by war? They would have not been able to get to safety. I often wonder what happened to them. They'd clearly been raped, abused, sold into slavery in one way or another. It's doubtful that any of them would ever have been rescued or escaped. Even if they did get back home somehow, the lifelong physical and emotional scars they'd suffered would make their later life a post-traumatic living hell. Perhaps I was the last person other than a rapist that the girl who caught my eye ever saw. It still sends a shudder through my body whenever I think of it. I can make a difference. Maybe not to that specific girl, but to hundreds of girls and boys whose stories involve cross-border abduction.

The responsibility weighs heavily on me. I've seen what happens when nobody can help. In these situations, I can help. If I sit back and do nothing, some kid's going to be brought up by terrorists or worse. I'm one of the very few people in the world who can do this. There are maybe, out of almost 8 billion people in the world, just a hundred thousand private military contractors. Of those, I could almost count on the fingers of one hand those who've developed the necessary skills and do child recovery. I do this because I must do this.

For every case I'm able to take on, I'll find myself turning down ten more because I simply don't have the resources. I'd love to expand. I'd love to develop my company, training up many more field operatives. I'd love to be able to find ways of raising money, so that the costs of an operation could be covered by benefactors rather than placing a burden on the person who just wants to get their child back. I've seen the cowboys in this industry who'll charge the earth and deliver nothing. It leaves me with a massive sense of responsibility.

There's a strange dichotomy. On the one hand, I dream of the day when I can simply come home and stay home with my wife and family. On the other hand, I never feel so alive as I do when I'm following my passion and doing the things I believe I was always meant to do. To me, there's a sense of destiny about working in child recovery. Things happen for a reason, and the way everything just fell into place merely confirms that I am where I'm supposed to be. I feel a pure passion in my soul which drives me on. It is a compulsion. I cannot stand by and let these things happen without doing everything in my power to save these boys and girls from parents who have evil intent.

Barely a day goes by where I don't see an article in a newspaper, online or on television about kids going missing. Whenever I see yet another example of this tragedy, it has a physical effect on me. There's a tension, a physical feeling which I can only describe as a sickly knot in my stomach, when it happens. My soul wants to jump out of my body and fix everything, but I'm completely restricted by the unfortunate essence of being human, and the inconvenient laws of physics.

I remember an incident from back in my private contracting days. A client was so terrified of being killed on the dangerous, war-torn roads, that he would hug every member of the team when we'd managed to drop him off safely at his destination. The penny still didn't drop. It was only when we received a video email from him, months later, that I started to understand the impact our missions could have on real families, real people's lives. The video showed his young daughter, thanking us for the fact her dad had made it safely home. That was the first time I'd ever seen any real appreciation for what we do, at least from a client. Awards from the military - medals, coins and certificates – mean nothing to me. They're just physical trinkets and tokens. I don't attach sentimental value to objects in that way. I attach value to people. That's what really hit home to me: the thought that a little girl could have grown up without her dad if our mission had failed.

The more time that passes, the more I find myself dwelling on those incidents. For years, I'd repressed my emotions because of the way my own father treated me. In the Army, I kept my emotions to myself because they weren't part of being a soldier. Even whilst contracting, as I started to come back alive, I still had a calm indifference at times. Then, the floodgates of emotion came in.

It's taken many years for me to be able to process those emotions in a way that I can put down on paper. With age, and maturity, I can finally begin to understand how I should have perceived things all along.

Most of all though, it's about the people. My biggest regret from that Lebanon mission is that I can't get in touch with Pieter and say a simple 'thank you' for all his help, support and belief in me. I wouldn't know how to find him now, and it's not exactly as though I can go into Lebanon and look for him. I stayed away from Sarah for years, not wanting to take the risk of getting in touch until sufficient time had passed for me to feel safe doing so. Then, last year, whilst I was back out in Afghanistan, we finally got back in contact. After exchanging a few emails, we made contact by phone.

Sarah put her daughter on the line, explaining to her that I'm the person who helped them get out of Lebanon. "Thank you", her daughter said to me in the most beautiful English. Thinking back now, I wonder whether they were the first words she'd ever spoken to me: she had been so quiet during the rescue.

There's my answer, in a nutshell. In just those two words, I could see my life's purpose so clearly. Thank you. Hearing those words, from the girl I'd rescued, meant the absolute world to me. It touched my heart, bringing all those emotions which I rarely feel flooding to the fore at once. I had a frog in my throat and a tear in my eye.

I know that whatever I do, I won't be able to change the whole world. All I can do is intervene to protect one little girl's life, and then another – and another. That 'thank you' is my motivation, and that is the one memory I know I'll keep with me until the day I die.